# So You Think You're A Sports Fan?!

# So You Think You're A Sports Fan?!

## The Ultimate Sports Quiz Game Book

## SPO PRODUCTIONS

WALKER AND COMPANY ✺ NEW YORK

First published in the United States of America in 1994 by Walker
Publishing Company, Inc.

Published simultaneously in Canada by Thomas Allen & Son Canada,
Limited, Markham, Ontario

Library of Congress Cataloging-in-Publication Data
So you think you're a sports fan?! : the ultimate sports quiz game book
/ SPO Productions.
p.  cm.
ISBN 0-8027-7439-3 (pbk.)
1. Sports—Miscellanea.  I. SPO Productions.
GV706.8.S6  1994
796'.02—dc20        94-31927
CIP

Book design by Ron Monteleone

Printed in the United States of America

2  4  6  8  10  9  7  5  3  1

# CONTENTS

# ACKNOWLEDGMENTS

WITHOUT THE FRIENDSHIP AND HARD WORK OF TOM ODJAK-JIAN, DAVID BROWN, JULIO GOMEZ, AND RICH ROSE, THIS BOOK WOULD NOT HAVE BEEN POSSIBLE.

SPECIAL THANKS GO TO THE PEOPLE WHO PUT IN THE ALL-NIGHTERS AND CREATIVE ENERGY TO MOLD THE FUN AND INTRIGUE THAT MAKES "THE DREAM LEAGUE" SUCH A SUCCESS. MOST NOTABLY, THANKS GO TO RESEARCHER GEOFF STRAIN, TO THE FAST FINGERS AND TIRELESS SUPPORT OF RODNIE NELSON AND SKIP WALSH, TO DOUG WOOLLEY FOR HIS KNOWLEDGE, ENTHUSIASM, AND

**acknowledgments**

MUCH NEEDED HUMOR, AND TO JOHN WILLIAMS, WHOSE SUPPORT HAS FACILITATED MUCH OF SPO'S PROGRESS AND SUCCESS.

FINALLY, THIS BOOK IS DEDICATED TO FANS OF "THE DREAM LEAGUE" AND FRUSTRATED JOCKS EVERYWHERE.

**S**O YOU THINK YOU'RE A SPORTS FAN?!

# INTRODUCTION

Before you dive into the question-and-answer sections that make up about 99 percent of this book, we recommend that you take at least a minute or two to read this introduction and familiarize yourself with the book's layout and methodology. If you don't, you may be hopelessly confused by things like "Extra Point" questions, the answers to which are nowhere to be found in the book, and "Time Trials," which are races against the clock in which you must keep track of your cumulative times from chapter to chapter.

In a nutshell, this book is based on the television program "The Dream League," a sports-trivia game show that airs on ESPN. Virtually every question in the book has been asked on the show in one form or another (although we did have to make up a few new questions to round out some of the chapters), and the book as a whole has been designed to mimic the feel of the show in general: fast-paced, informative, and most of all, fun.

The book begins with a 100-question "Sports Literacy Test," which is billed as 100 questions that every true sports fan should be able to answer. These aren't the 100 easiest questions in the world, nor are they the 100 most popular. Instead, they're designed to test your basic knowledge in a wide variety of sports subjects, and if you're not a well-rounded sports fan, you're going to run into trouble right away.

The Sports Literacy Test is followed by ten 50-question "challenges," each of which revolves around some central theme, such as nicknames, unsung heroes, and famous firsts. Each challenge's theme is broad enough that the questions within it can jump from sport to sport and era to era (just as they do on the actual show), so if your sports knowledge is limited to baseball, or the 1950s, or Cleveland, watch out. The answers are located in the Answers section, and each challenge also contains its own scoring key that will allow you to track your progress throughout the book, as well as compare your own scores to those of your friends.

Within each challenge, the 50 questions are fairly straightforward. You either know the answer or you don't, and you score points accordingly, one for each correct answer, with no partial credit awarded. Included in each challenge, however, are two additional "bonus" sections that do require some explanation.

One of the biggest differences between answering questions out of a book, as opposed to competing against another contestant with the television cameras rolling, is the time factor. When you're a contestant on "The Dream League," you don't just have to know the answer, you have to know it faster than your opponent. So to give readers a sense of what it's like answering questions under the gun, we've added what we call a "Time Trial" to each challenge, a 10-to-15-question "sprint" that is designed to be completed in anywhere from one to two minutes.

Each time trial is related in some way to the larger theme of the challenge, but instead of answering the questions at your leisure, you're given a specific length of time in which you're expected to complete the trial. You are also penalized for each incorrect answer, usually five seconds per mistake. Together, the 10 Time Trials make up sort of a sports-trivia decathlon, and by keeping track of your total time from chapter to chapter, you can track your progress from event to event. If you finish all 10 in less than 15 minutes, you're in the money, but you'll need to finish in under 12 minutes to walk away with the gold.

Each challenge concludes with an "Extra Point" question, the answer to which cannot be found anywhere in the book. If you've ever watched "The Dream League," you know that after each round, the team that is leading is given an opportunity to earn

"Extra Points" by successfully completing a physical sports challenge such as throwing footballs at a target or shooting a basketball three-pointer. Unfortunately, it's rather difficult to re-create such "hands-on" challenges in a book format, so we were forced to come up with the next-best thing—a contest.

To enter, write down your answers to all of the extra point questions. (You must have answers to all of the questions or your entry will be invalidated.) Mail your entry, complete with your name, address, and daytime phone number, to:

SPORTS FAN CONTEST
c/o Walker and Company
435 Hudson Street
New York, NY 10014

If you have all of the answers correct, your entry will go into the SPORTS FAN CONTEST DRAWING. All entries must be received by May 31, 1995. (No phone calls, please.)

Three Grand Prize Winners will be notified by June 30, 1995. The winners will each receive their very own personalized Official Dream League jersey usually awarded to contestants on "The Dream League." These jerseys, which have a retail value of $300, are not available in stores.

Let the games begin!

# $\mathbb{S}$PORTS LITERACY TEST

SO YOU THINK YOU'RE A SPORTS FAN, HUH? IF YOU'RE READING THIS BOOK, YOU PROBABLY DO. NOW HERE'S YOUR FIRST CHANCE TO PROVE IT. OUR SPORTS LITERACY TEST CONSISTS OF 100 QUESTIONS THAT WE THINK EVERY *TRUE* SPORTS FAN SHOULD KNOW THE ANSWERS TO. THEY AREN'T THE 100 EASIEST QUESTIONS IN THE WORLD, HOWEVER. IN FACT, SOME OF THEM ARE QUITE HARD. BUT IF YOU'RE REALLY A SPORTS FAN, YOU SHOULD BE UP TO THE CHALLENGE. IF NOT, THE ANSWERS BEGIN ON PAGE 75.

1. Who was the last baseball player to bat .400 for an entire season?

2. Name the only player to win the Heisman Trophy twice.

3. Which two conferences' champions play in the Rose Bowl?

4. Which current NHL teams make up the "Original Six"?

5. In baseball, who hit the "Shot Heard 'Round the World"?

6. What horse won the Belmont Stakes by an incredible 31 lengths in 1973?

7. In which event did Dick Fosbury win the gold medal at the 1968 Summer Olympics?

8. Which NBA team has won the most world championships?

9. What baseball team featured the double-play combination of Tinker, Evers, and Chance?

10. What two teams met in Super Bowl I?

11. Name the three weapons used in fencing.

12. Who broke the four-minute barrier in the mile run?

13. In the poem "Casey at the Bat," what team did Casey play for?

14. Who fought in the "Thrilla in Manilla"?

15. What legendary basketball team was founded by Abe Saperstein in 1927?

16. What sport awards the Hobey Baker Award?

17. In basketball, who holds the NCAA single-season scoring average record?

18 Who coached UCLA to a record seven consecutive NCAA basketball championships from 1967 to 1973?

19 Between 1964 and 1973, name the only school besides UCLA to win the NCAA basketball championship.

20 In baseball, what two players make up "the battery"?

21 Name the only American to win bicycling's Tour de France.

22 What does a baseball player have to do to achieve "the cycle"?

23 Who won the first Heisman Trophy?

24 Who was baseball's first commissioner?

25 Who kicked the longest field goal in NFL history?

26 What was the final score of the 1940 NFL Championship Game?

27 How many home runs did Hank Aaron hit in his major league career?

28 What Japanese slugger broke Hank Aaron's professional home-run record in 1977?

29 What major sporting event takes place each year in Augusta, Georgia?

30 What were the nicknames of Army backfield stars Doc Blanchard and Glenn Davis?

31 What three events make up Hawaii's annual "Ironman Triathlon"?

32 Who holds baseball's single-season home-run record, and how many did he hit?

33 Who holds the NBA record for points in one game, and how many did he score?

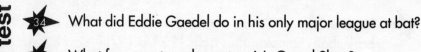

34 ► What did Eddie Gaedel do in his only major league at bat?

35 ► What four events make up tennis's Grand Slam?

36 ► What four events make up golf's Grand Slam?

37 ► In order, what three races make up thoroughbred racing's Triple Crown?

38 ► In baseball, what three offensive categories make up the Triple Crown?

39 ► Entering the 1994 season, name the last baseball player to win the Triple Crown.

40 ► Who was Abner Doubleday?

41 ► Who invented basketball?

42 ► Whose general "rules" govern the sport of boxing?

43 ► Name two of the five countries that have won soccer's World Cup more than once.

44 ► Name the only pitcher to throw a no-hitter in the World Series.

45 ► What swimmer won seven gold medals at the 1972 Summer Olympics?

46 ► Who was the first NHL player to score 50 goals in one season?

47 ► Who holds the longest hitting streak in baseball history?

48 ► Name the only school to win both the NCAA and NIT basketball championships during the same season.

49 ► What football team featured the "Four Horsemen"?

50 ► What football team featured the "Fearsome Foursome"?

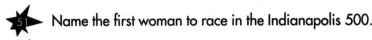

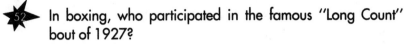

51 ► Name the first woman to race in the Indianapolis 500.

52 ► In boxing, who participated in the famous "Long Count" bout of 1927?

53 ► Where would one find the "Green Monster"?

54 ► What did Roy Reigels do in the 1929 Rose Bowl?

55 ► Which schools make up Philadelphia's "Big Five"?

56 ► Name the NFL's all-time scoring leader.

57 ► Name the NBA's all-time scoring leader.

58 ► Name the NHL's all-time goals leader.

59 ► Name major league baseball's all-time leader in runs scored.

60 ► Name the two different gaits run by horses in harness racing.

61 ► In 1974, what school broke UCLA's incredible 88-game winning streak in men's basketball?

62 ► According to ancient Greek legend, who "won" the first marathon?

63 ► Name the two Heisman Trophy winners who played for Donald Trump's New Jersey Generals in the USFL.

64 ► At the Winter Olympics, what two sports make up the biathlon?

65 ► Who shattered the world record by long-jumping 29 feet, 2$^1/_2$ inches at the 1968 Summer Olympics?

66 ► Name the only AFL team to win the Super Bowl.

67 ► Name the only NFL team to go undefeated for an entire season, including the Super Bowl.

68 ► In 1973, who competed in tennis's "Battle of the Sexes"?

69 ► Where is the annual Soap Box Derby held?

70 ► What is a hat trick?

71 ► What is the final event of the decathlon?

72 ► Who wrote *Ball Four*?

73 ► Who won four consecutive Olympic gold medals in the discus from 1956 to 1968?

74 ► Name the 1940 NFL rushing champion who eventually found a seat on the United States Supreme Court.

75 ► What eastern city is home to the Little League World Series?

76 ► What western state is home to the Iditarod?

77 ► What is the traditional victory drink at the Indianapolis 500?

78 ► Who scored the "Hand of God" goal that defeated England in the semifinals of the 1986 World Cup?

79 ► Whom did Bobby Fischer defeat to capture the World Chess Championship in 1972?

80 ► Nolan Ryan holds the major league record with seven career no-hitters. Who is second?

81 ► Who was the youngest boxer to win a world heavyweight championship?

82 ► Which two American sprinters caused a scandal with their "black power" salute at the 1968 Summer Olympics?

83 ► Besides Shoeless Joe Jackson, name one other member of the "Black Sox."

84 ► What is the Olympic motto?

What player owns the highest career scoring average in NBA history?

 In the 1972 AFC playoffs, who made the "Immaculate Reception"?

 In the 1981 NFC Championship Game, who made "The Catch"?

 Whose picture appears on the world's most valuable baseball card?

 What gymnast recorded seven perfect scores of 10 at the 1976 Summer Olympics?

 Name one of the legendary running backs who wore number 44 for Syracuse University.

 Who broke baseball's color barrier?

 What position did Babe Ruth play in his first major league game?

 What Norwegian figure skater won three Olympic gold medals before embarking on a successful Hollywood film career?

 In bowling, what is a "turkey"?

 Name the last NCAA Division I men's basketball champion to finish the season with a perfect record.

 On February 25, 1964, who defeated Sonny Liston to win the world heavyweight boxing championship?

 What former Dallas Cowboy was once "The World's Fastest Human"?

 What is Johnny Vander Meer's claim to fame?

 How many horses have won the Kentucky Derby twice?

 What is a Zamboni?

# CHALLENGE 1.

## BACK TO SCHOOL

FROM CHAPEL HILL, NORTH CAROLINA, TO CORVALLIS, OREGON, INTERCOLLEGIATE ATHLETICS ARE SECOND TO NONE WHEN IT COMES TO IGNITING SPORTS FANS' PASSIONS. BUT IF YOU CONSIDER YOURSELF A COLLEGE SPORTS AFICIONADO, HERE ARE 50 CAMPUS-RELATED QUESTIONS THAT WILL LET YOU FIND OUT JUST HOW WELL YOU'VE BEEN STUDYING. IF YOU CAN ANSWER ONLY 25 OR FEWER, YOU'RE HEADED FOR THE JUNIOR VARSITY, BUT 35 WILL EARN YOU A LETTER. IF YOU GET 45 RIGHT, YOU'RE HEADED FOR THE PROS, AND IF YOU ACE ALL

50 CONSIDER YOURSELF AN ALL-AMERICAN. THE ANSWERS BEGIN ON

PAGE 83.

 In college football, who competes in the Amos Alonzo Stagg Bowl?

 Dean Smith has won two NCAA basketball championships as the head coach of the University of North Carolina, and each time, the Final Four was played in the same arena. Name it.

 What Oklahoma star won the Heisman Trophy as a junior in 1978, then placed second in the voting as a senior in 1979?

 In 1981, which two teams played in the last Final Four consolation game?

 What school has won the most NCAA Division I women's basketball championships?

 What school won ten consecutive NCAA championships in indoor track from 1984 to 1993?

 Usually thought of as a basketball power, what ACC school won eight straight national championships in women's soccer from 1986 to 1993?

 What Big Ten school won nine consecutive NCAA wrestling titles from 1978 to 1986?

 What state would you be in if you were playing at Seton Hall?

 What southern school produced the Most Valuable Player in each of the first three Super Bowls?

 What school was the lowest seed ever to win the NCAA men's basketball tournament?

What school won the NCAA men's basketball championship with a record-high 11 losses during the regular season?

 Name the only school to reach the NCAA men's basketball championship game in its only tournament appearance.

 Name the only college to produce two NFL Rookie of the Year winners during the 1980s.

 Which college basketball coach was the first to win at least 100 games at three different schools—specifically, North Carolina, South Carolina, and St. John's?

# T I M E (00:00) T R I A L

Listed below are the 12 members of the 1992 U.S. Olympic basketball "Dream Team," the 12 colleges they attended, and the 11 nicknames (two schools share the same nickname) of those schools' athletic teams. How quickly can you match each player to his alma mater, and each school to the appropriate nickname? In this event, your target time is 1:30, with a five-second penalty for each incorrect answer.

| | | |
|---|---|---|
| Charles Barkley | Auburn | Bears |
| Larry Bird | Central Arkansas | Blue Devils |
| Clyde Drexler | Duke | Bulldogs |
| Patrick Ewing | Georgetown | Cougars |
| Magic Johnson | Gonzaga | Hoyas |
| Michael Jordan | Houston | Midshipmen |
| Christian Laettner | Indiana State | Redmen |
| Karl Malone | Louisiana Tech | Spartans |
| Chris Mullin | Michigan State | Sycamores |
| Scottie Pippen | Navy | Tar Heels |
| David Robinson | North Carolina | Tigers |
| John Stockton | St. John's | |

**Answers:** Charles Barkley (Auburn Tigers), Larry Bird (Indiana State Sycamores), Clyde Drexler (Houston Cougars), Patrick Ewing (Georgetown Hoyas), Magic Johnson (Michigan State Spartans), Michael Jordan (North Carolina Tar Heels), Christian Laettner (Duke Blue Devils), Karl Malone (Louisiana Tech Bulldogs), Chris Mullin (St. John's Redmen), Scottie Pippen (Central Arkansas Bears), David Robinson (Navy Midshipmen), John Stockton (Gonzaga Bulldogs)

What do Walter Dukes (who played college basketball at Seton Hall), Bill Russell (San Francisco), Paul Silas (Creighton), Julius Erving (Massachusetts), Artis Gilmore (Jacksonville), and Kermit Washington (American) have in common?

 What do Moses Malone, Bill Willoughby, and Daryl Dawkins have in common?

 Name the last service academy player to win the Heisman Trophy.

 What school won the first Rose Bowl?

 Which school has won the most Rose Bowls?

 What Pac-10 school is the only one to win the NCAA championship in both men's and women's basketball?

 What UCLA center once scored 44 points in the NCAA men's basketball championship game?

 What UCLA center is the only player to be named MVP of three consecutive NCAA basketball tournaments?

 What school did Bud Wilkinson coach to three national championships in football during the 1950s?

 Only three Division I football players have ever rushed for more than 2,000 yards in a single season. Name any one of them.

 What midwestern city is home to baseball's College World Series?

 What current Pac-10 team won the first NCAA basketball tournament in 1939?

 Louisiana State's Pete Maravich holds the NCAA record for most points in one basketball season with 1,381 in 1969–

70. What former University of Houston star is second all-time with 1,214?

 In addition to holding the single-season scoring record, Pete Maravich is one of only two players to win three NCAA scoring championships. Name the University of Cincinnati star who also accomplished that feat.

 Entering the 1994 season, who was the last Pac-10 player to win the Heisman Trophy?

 Who won the Heisman Trophy in 1968 after finishing second to crosstown rival Gary Beban the year before?

 What eastern school once featured the "Seven Blocks of Granite"?

 What Big Ten school produced both Jack Nicklaus and John Havlicek?

 Although it hasn't won the title since 1978, what school has won the College World Series the most times?

 If you were an Explorer, what Pennsylvania school would you play for?

 If Duke's teams are called the Blue Devils, what is the nickname of teams from Duquesne?

 What former Notre Dame star set an NCAA tournament record with 61 points against Ohio University in 1970?

 Before leading the U.S. Olympic hockey team to the gold medal in 1980, what school did Herb Brooks lead to three NCAA hockey championships?

 Brigham Young University is known for producing outstanding quarterbacks, but can you name the only BYU quarterback to start in a Super Bowl?

What former Oakland Raider boasted of graduating from "The University of Mars"?

 What conference features the University of Akron, Ball State, Kent State, and Ohio University?

 In college football history, the University of Oklahoma, the University of Texas, and Army all had winning streaks of at least 25 games broken by the same school. Name it.

 In 1990, what school set an NCAA men's basketball tournament record with 149 points in one game less than two weeks after their leading scorer died of a heart attack?

 With seven Heisman Trophies, Notre Dame players have won more than any other school. Name at least three of Notre Dame's Heisman winners.

 Bobby Bowden coached Florida State to college football's national championship in 1993, but his son, Terry, actually posted a better record that year. What southern school did the younger Bowden coach?

 Who coached Notre Dame to four national championships in football from 1943 to 1949?

 What Southeastern Conference school's mascot is a bulldog named "UGA"?

 In 1993, the only two-time MVP of the NCAA women's basketball tournament became head coach at her alma mater. Name her.

 On the television series "Coach," what school does the title character work for?

 Name the last Ivy League school to play in a college football bowl game.

**EXTRA POINT**

Name the only Division I school to win an NCAA championship in all four major men's sports: football, baseball, basketball, and hockey.

# CHALLENGE 2.

# IN THE BEGINNING

NOW THAT YOU'VE BRUSHED UP ON YOUR COLLEGE SPORTS KNOWLEDGE, IT'S TIME TO MOVE ON TO THE PROS, AND WHERE BETTER TO START THAN "IN THE BEGINNING"? IN THIS CHAPTER, ALL 50 QUESTIONS PERTAIN TO THE "EARLY YEARS" OF FAMOUS TEAMS, PLAYERS, COACHES, AND LEAGUES. IF YOU GUESS RIGHT ON 35 OR MORE, YOU'RE OFF TO A GOOD START, BUT IF YOU CAN ONLY ANSWER 25, YOU SHOULD PROBABLY START WORRYING. IF YOU CONNECT ON 45 OUT OF 50, IT COULD BE THE START OF SOMETHING BIG, AND A PERFECT 50 MEANS

YOU'VE EARNED ROOKIE OF THE YEAR. THE ANSWERS BEGIN ON

PAGE 87.

---

 What city once fielded a major league baseball team called the Pilots?

 Who coached the Baltimore Colts to their first Super Bowl appearance?

 Before joining the NHL, what current Western Conference team won the last two World Hockey Association championships in 1978 and 1979?

 Name the other three NHL teams which were once members of the WHA.

 Which two American League teams were once called the Washington Senators?

 What team did Earl Monroe play for when he made his NBA debut in 1967?

 What position did Jackie Robinson play during his first major league season?

 Eight years before coaching Mary Lou Retton to an Olympic gold medal in 1984, Bela Karolyi guided another legendary gymnast to gold in Montreal. Name her.

 In 1991, at what Grand Slam event did golfer John Daly record his first career tour victory?

 What NFL team drafted Auburn's Bo Jackson with the first pick overall in the 1986 draft?

 In what stadium did the New York Mets play their first home game?

Name Wayne Gretzky's first professional hockey team.

 At what New England school did Rick Pitino begin his college basketball head coaching career?

 John Wooden is best known for coaching the UCLA basketball team from 1949 to 1975, but what midwestern school did Wooden coach before joining the Bruins?

 Wooden was also an accomplished player before embark-

# T I M E ⏱ (00:00) T R I A L

In baseball and basketball, players often change teams several times before finally finding success. In this event, you have 1:15 to match the players from the column on the left to the team that originally drafted (or signed) him from the column on the right. Remember, though, that some of the players were traded before they ever played for the team in question. Again, add five seconds to your time for selecting the wrong team, but in this event, there's an additional five-second penalty for selecting the wrong sport.

| | |
|---|---|
| Roberto Alomar | Chicago Cubs |
| Mookie Blaylock | Cleveland Cavaliers |
| Muggsy Bogues | Indiana Pacers |
| Joe Carter | Los Angeles Dodgers |
| Andre Dawson | Montreal Expos |
| Kevin Johnson | New Jersey Nets |
| Fred McGriff | New York Yankees |
| Scottie Pippen | Philadelphia Phillies |
| Ryne Sandberg | San Diego Padres |
| Dave Stewart | Seattle Supersonics |
| Wayman Tisdale | Utah Jazz |
| Dominique Wilkins | Washington Bullets |

**Answers:** Roberto Alomar (San Diego Padres), Mookie Blaylock (New Jersey Nets), Muggsy Bogues (Washington Bullets), Joe Carter (Chicago Cubs), Andre Dawson (Montreal Expos), Kevin Johnson (Cleveland Cavaliers), Fred McGriff (New York Yankees), Scottie Pippen (Seattle Supersonics), Dave Stewart (Los Angeles Dodgers), Ryne Sandberg (Philadelphia Phillies), Wayman Tisdale (Indiana Pacers), Dominique Wilkins (Utah Jazz)

ing on his legendary coaching career. At what midwestern school did he star?

 Since moving from Brooklyn to Los Angeles in 1958, the Dodgers have had only two managers. Who was their first L.A. skipper?

 Where did the NFL's Rams play before moving to Los Angeles in 1946?

 Which two current NFL teams used to play their home games at Kezar Stadium?

 What current NFC East team played its home games at Boston's Fenway Park from 1933 to 1936?

 What New York City high school did Lew Alcindor attend?

 What NBA Hall of Famer attended Overbrook High School in Philadelphia?

 At what service academy did Bobby Knight coach prior to his successful tenure at Indiana?

 What NFL legend was the head coach of the Dallas Cowboys during their inaugural season?

 What current NFL head coach once won back-to-back championships in the USFL?

 What two cities were home to the Athletics before they moved to Oakland in 1968?

 Name three of the six teams that joined the NHL in 1967, when the size of the league doubled from six teams to twelve.

 Which NHL expansion team reached the Stanley Cup finals that year?

 In the NBA, what southern city was home to the Jazz before they moved to Utah in 1980?

What current NFC East team was originally based in Chicago when it joined the NFL in 1920?

 At what SEC school did New York Knicks coach Pat Riley earn All-America honors as a player during the 1960s?

 The Heisman Trophy is named for former college football coach John Heisman. What school is he most famous for coaching?

 What Great Lakes city did the Sacramento Kings originally call home?

 Which four NBA teams were originally members of the American Basketball Association?

 What major league baseball team did Danny Ainge once play for?

 With what team did Deion Sanders make his major league debut?

 With what team did Reggie Jackson make his major league debut?

 With what team did Babe Ruth make his major league debut?

 In 1976, when the coach of the expansion Tampa Bay Buccaneers was asked about his hapless team's execution, he allegedly replied, "I'm all for it!" Name him.

 Former Baltimore Colts coach Don McCafferty is one of only two NFL coaches to win the Super Bowl in their rookie season. Who was the other?

 Before being traded to the Philadelphia Flyers, Eric Lindros sat out the entire 1991–92 hockey season, refusing to play for the team that drafted him. Name Lindros's "original" team.

41 What current NBA team once played its home games in Buffalo, New York?

 42 During the 1970s, the NBA's Buffalo Braves produced three Rookie of the Year Award winners. Name two of them.

 43 During his 24-year managerial career, Leo Durocher skippered the Giants, Dodgers, Cubs, and Astros. Which team did he manage first?

 44 Where did Ara Parseghian last coach before moving on to Notre Dame in 1964?

 45 What NFL team did Notre Dame's Lou Holtz once coach?

 46 Before switching to silver and black, what were the original colors of the NHL's Los Angeles Kings?

 47 What college did Dallas Cowboys quarterback Troy Aikman attend before transferring to UCLA?

 48 Nolan Ryan reached the World Series only once during his 27-year career, and it came in his third season in the majors. What team did Ryan play for that year?

 49 What expansion team joined the American Football League in 1966?

 50 Of the four Grand Slam events in tennis, which one is the oldest?

EXTRA POINT

What current American League city was the original home of the New York Yankees?

# CHALLENGE 3.

## FAMOUS FIRSTS

👉 IN SPORTS, RECORDS ARE MADE TO BE BROKEN, BUT WHEN YOU'RE THE FIRST TO ACCOMPLISH A CERTAIN FEAT, NO ONE CAN EVER TAKE THAT AWAY. IN THIS CHAPTER, ALL 50 QUESTIONS HONOR THOSE ATHLETES WHO BOLDLY WENT WHERE NONE HAD GONE BEFORE, AND IF YOU CAN'T ANSWER MORE THAN 25 OF THEM, YOU COULD PROBABLY USE SOME FIRST AID. THIRTY-FIVE OUT OF 50 WILL EARN YOU FIRST RUNNER-UP, WHILE 45 WILL MAKE YOU A FIRST-ROUND DRAFT PICK. AND IF YOU CAN ANSWER ALL 50, YOU'LL BE SITTING PRETTY IN FIRST PLACE. ANSWERS BEGIN ON PAGE 92.

Who won baseball's first World Series?

 Who scored the first touchdown in Super Bowl history?

 In 1869, what city became the home of the first all-professional baseball team?

 What major sporting event was first held at Chamonix, France, in 1924?

 What major sporting event takes place each year on the first Saturday of May?

 In hockey, what piece of equipment was Jacques Plante the first to use regularly?

 In 1936, who was the first pick overall in the first NFL draft?

 Oddly, who was the first golfer to reach $1 million in earnings in a single year?

 In baseball, each league's Rookie of the Year receives the Jackie Robinson Award. Who was baseball's first Rookie of the Year?

 Who was the first African-American player in the American League?

 Name the first U.S. city to host the Olympics.

 In 1935, Babe Ruth, Ty Cobb, Walter Johnson, Christy Mathewson, and Honus Wagner became the first players to be inducted into baseball's Hall of Fame. Which of those legends received the most votes?

 In boxing, who was the first heavyweight champion to reclaim the title after losing it?

 Who was the first designated hitter in major league history?

At the 1993 U.S. Open, who became the first golfer ever to reach Baltusrol's 17th green in just two shots?

 Who was the first player from USC to win college football's Heisman Trophy?

 What USC Heisman Trophy winner was the first college football player to rush for more than 2,000 yards in a single season?

 On April 8, 1993, who became the first player ever to hit one home run from each side of the plate in the same inning?

## T I M E 00:00 T R I A L

If you've been paying attention so far, at least half of this time trial should be a breeze. Simply put these 12 major sporting events in chronological order by matching them to the years in which they were first held. Your goal should be to finish in under one minute, but don't forget to add five seconds to your time for each one you get wrong.

| | |
|---|---|
| The World Series | 1875 |
| The Super Bowl | 1877 |
| The Stanley Cup | 1895 |
| The NBA Finals | 1896 |
| The Summer Olympics | 1903 |
| The Winter Olympics | 1918 |
| The U.S. Open (golf) | 1924 |
| Wimbledon | 1930 |
| The Kentucky Derby | 1933 |
| The Baseball All-Star Game | 1936 |
| The NFL Draft | 1947 |
| The World Cup | 1966 |

**Answers:** The Kentucky Derby (1875), Wimbledon (1877), The U.S. Open (1895), The Summer Olympics (1896), The World Series (1903), The Stanley Cup (1918), The Winter Olympics (1924), The World Cup (1930), The All-Star Game (1933), The NFL Draft (1936), The NBA Finals (1947), The Super Bowl (1966)

When the Orlando Magic defied the odds by winning the NBA's draft lottery two years in a row, whom did they select with their first picks?

 In what sporting event was Willy T. Ribbs the first African-American to compete?

 Who was the first African-American player to win a Wimbledon singles title?

 Who was the first African-American to win the world heavyweight boxing championship?

 Who won the ABA's first Most Valuable Player Award after being banned from the NBA for gambling?

 In baseball, who hit the first home run in All-Star competition?

 Who hit the first grand slam in All-Star competition?

 What Super Bowl coach was also the first tight end elected to the pro football Hall of Fame?

 Who was the first pure kicker to be inducted into the pro football Hall of Fame?

 What California track was the site of the first Breeder's Cup in 1984?

 When Michael Jordan was drafted by the Chicago Bulls in 1984, what University of Houston star was the first pick overall?

 Name the first NHL expansion team to win the Stanley Cup.

 In what Olympic event did Sweden's Ulrich Salchow win the first gold medal in 1908?

 At the 1984 All-Star Game, who won the NBA's first "Slam Dunk" contest?

Nicknamed "Little Mo," who was the first woman to win the Grand Slam in tennis?

 What former Lakers star was the first commissioner of the American Basketball Association?

 What notorious figure skater was the first American woman to complete a triple axel in competition?

 In 1994, what Big 10 school became the first non-California team ever to win the NCAA Division I men's volleyball championship?

 Name the first female jockey to win a Triple Crown race.

 What did the Philadelphia Flyers' Ron Hextall do on December 8, 1987?

 In 1964, who became the first American to win an Olympic medal in skiing?

 What Boston Bruin was the first NHL player to score 100 points in a single season?

 In soccer, what South American country captured the first World Cup title with a 4–2 victory over Argentina in 1930?

 What University of Kentucky star was the Charlotte Hornets' first-ever draft pick?

 In addition to once being traded for Ozzie Smith, what switch-hitting shortstop was the first player ever to collect 100 hits from each side of the plate in the same season?

 In the 1960 season, what team did George Blanda quarterback to the first-ever AFL championship?

 In 1948, which NFL team became the first to put emblems on its helmets?

**46** In 1987, which cable television network became the first to broadcast an NFL game?

 **47** Where was the first indoor Super Bowl played?

 **48** Who was the first Little League alumnus to play in the major leagues?

 **49** In 1910, which President became the first to throw out a ceremonial "first pitch" on Opening Day?

 **50** What do the horses Aristides, Survivor, and Ruthless have in common?

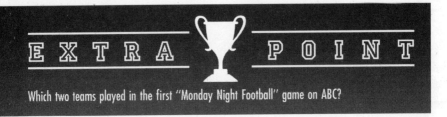

EXTRA POINT

Which two teams played in the first "Monday Night Football" game on ABC?

# CHALLENGE 4.

## WE HARDLY KNEW YE

IN THE WORLD OF MUSIC, THEY'RE CALLED "ONE-HIT WONDERS," UNKNOWN ARTISTS WHO SUDDENLY SOAR TO THE TOP OF THE CHARTS, THEN ARE NEVER HEARD FROM AGAIN. IN SPORTS, THEY'RE OFTEN CALLED "FLASHES IN THE PAN," AND WHILE THEY RARELY BECOME HOUSEHOLD NAMES, THEY ALL ENJOY A MEASURE OF IMMORTALITY. IN THIS CHAPTER, ALL 50 QUESTIONS FOCUS ON SOME OF THE SPORTS WORLD'S LESSER-KNOWN HEROES, AND IF YOU CAN'T NAME AT LEAST 25 OF THEM, YOU TOO DESERVE TO BE FORGOTTEN. ON THE OTHER HAND, IF YOU CAN NAME 40 OUT OF 50, YOU'LL

MAKE QUITE A NAME FOR YOURSELF, AND IF YOU CAN PUT TOGETHER A PERFECT SCORE, CONSIDER THIS YOUR MOMENT IN THE SUN. ANSWERS BEGIN ON PAGE 96.

---

 Before Lou Gehrig, who played first base for the New York Yankees?

 Who scored the winning basket when North Carolina State upset Houston to win the 1983 NCAA men's basketball championship?

 In college football, who scored the winning touchdown when Boston College defeated Miami, 47–45, in 1984?

 Besides Joe Theisman and Joe Montana, name the only other former Notre Dame quarterback to start in a Super Bowl.

 In 1968, who replaced Vince Lombardi as coach of the Green Bay Packers?

 What Redskin running back is the only player to rush for 200 yards in a single Super Bowl?

 Who was Harry Steinfeldt?

 What scoring innovation is Jim Van Allen credited with introducing to the sport of tennis?

 In boxing, who succeeded Joe Louis as heavyweight champion of the world?

 What former Laker holds the NBA record for blocked shots in one game?

 Name the only major league pitcher to pitch a no-hitter and hit two home runs in the same game.

What track-and-field barrier did Charley Dumas break in 1956?

 How was New York University halfback Ed Smith "immortalized" in 1935?

 Name the only player to play in the NCAA Division I men's basketball championship game for two different schools.

 What Chicago Cub infielder was killed in a plane crash in February 1964, less than two years after winning the National League Rookie of the Year award?

# T I M E  T R I A L

Listed below in the column on the left are the team nicknames of the twelve original United States Football League franchises. How quickly can you match them to the appropriate city or state in the column on the right? Once again, your target time is one minute, with a five-second penalty for each wrong answer, but this time you can also *deduct* ten seconds from your total if you know which team won the inaugural USFL championship game.

| | |
|---|---|
| Stars | Arizona |
| Breakers | Birmingham |
| Generals | Boston |
| Federals | Chicago |
| Bandits | Denver |
| Blitz | Los Angeles |
| Stallions | Michigan |
| Panthers | New Jersey |
| Express | Oakland |
| Invaders | Philadelphia |
| Wranglers | Tampa Bay |
| Gold | Washington |

**Answers:** Philadelphia Stars, Boston Breakers, New Jersey Generals, Washington Federals, Tampa Bay Bandits, Chicago Blitz, Birmingham Stallions, Michigan Panthers, Los Angeles Express, Oakland Invaders, Arizona Wranglers, and Denver Gold.
On July 17, 1983, the Michigan Panthers won the first USFL championship game, 24–22, over the Philadelphia Stars.

Name the only American gymnast to win a medal in the 1988 Summer Olympics.

 Name the only player to hit two home runs in one game twice in the same World Series.

 Besides their position, what do Art Kusnyer, Jeff Torborg, Mike Egan, Alan Ashby, Ellie Rodriguez, John Russell, and Mike Stanley have in common?

 During the 1959–60 NBA season, this player became the first forward ever to average more than 30 points per game, but still didn't lead the league in scoring. Name him.

 During his nine-year career, Jim Brown won eight NFL rushing titles. What Green Bay Packer won the title the only year that Brown did not?

 In game seven of the 1992 National League Championship Series, who delivered the ninth-inning pinch hit that sent the Atlanta Braves to the World Series?

 In 1984, football's Irving Fryar, basketball's Akeem Olajuwon, and hockey's Mario Lemieux were each chosen with the first pick overall in their sport's amateur draft. Whom did the Mets select with the first pick overall in the baseball draft that year?

 On July 18, 1921, Babe Ruth set a major league record when he slugged his 139th career home run. Who held the all-time home run record before Ruth?

 In 1946, who succeeded Jim Thorpe as commissioner of the National Football League?

 Fred Perry is the last player from what country to win the men's singles championship at Wimbledon?

 During the 1980s, Rickey Henderson won nine American League stolen base crowns. Name the only other American Leaguer to lead the league in steals during that decade.

Who won the National League Cy Young Award in 1989 despite winning only four games for the San Diego Padres?

 Billie Jean King is one of the world's most famous tennis players, but her brother was also an accomplished athlete, pitching twelve years in the major leagues. Name him.

 In 1970, the New Orleans Saints' Joe Scarpati helped make history in a game against the Detroit Lions. How?

 What "feat" guaranteed Kansas City's Mike Mercer a permanent place in the Super Bowl record book?

 Fulton Walker and Stanford Jennings are the only two players to accomplish what feat in a Super Bowl?

 San Francisco's Jerry Rice is one of only two players to catch 11 passes in a single Super Bowl. Name the other.

 What Houston Astro suffered a career-ending stroke in 1980, just three weeks after starting for the National League in the All-Star Game?

 What was so remarkable about Eddie Eagan's gold medal for the United States in the four-man bobsled at the 1992 Winter Olympics?

 During the 1994–95 season, Lenny Wilkens should set the NBA record for most games coached. Whose record will he break?

 What boxer handed Mike Tyson his only loss as a professional?

 What team did Babe Ruth finish his major league career with?

 What NHL team did Bobby Orr finish his career with?

 What team did Vince Lombardi coach in his final NFL game?

we hardly knew ye

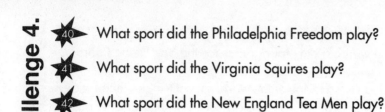

40 → What sport did the Philadelphia Freedom play?

41 → What sport did the Virginia Squires play?

42 → What sport did the New England Tea Men play?

43 → Entering the 1994 season, who was the last National League player to hit 50 home runs in one season?

44 → Who was the last manager to lead the New York Yankees to a World Series title?

45 → In what track-and-field event is Bob Richards the only man to win two Olympic gold medals?

46 → On July 9, 1969, who broke up Tom Seaver's bid for a perfect game with a one-out single in the ninth inning?

47 → In addition to playing goaltender for the Boston Bruins, what author once played quarterback for the Detroit Lions?

48 → What courageous but inexperienced Englishman finished last in the 70-meter ski jump in the 1988 Winter Olympics?

49 → What is Bobo Holloman's claim to fame?

50 → What is Vinko Bogataj's claim to fame?

# EXTRA POINT

Who scored the winning touchdown on California's famous five-lateral kickoff return against Stanford in 1982?

# CHALLENGE 5.

## BROKEN RECORDS

TO SPORTS FANS, FEW THINGS ARE MORE EXCITING THAN AN ATHLETE IN PURSUIT OF A RECORD, SO IN THIS CHAPTER, WE'VE BROUGHT TOGETHER 50 OF THE SPORTS WORLD'S MOST NOTABLE PERFORMANCES. SOME WERE ACHIEVED BY INDIVIDUALS, OTHERS BY TEAMS, BUT ALL ARE RECOGNIZED AS THE BEST (OR WORST) OF ALL TIME. HERE, 45 RIGHT ANSWERS PUTS YOU ON RECORD PACE, WHILE 35 EARNS YOU A NOTE WITH AN ASTERISK. IF YOU CAN'T ANSWER 25, YOU MAY WELL SET THE MARK FOR FUTILITY, BUT IF YOU SOMEHOW MANAGE TO ANSWER

---

 Who holds the NFL record for most career rushing touchdowns?

 Who holds the NHL record with 92 goals in one season?

 Whose long-standing record did Mike Powell break when he long-jumped 29 feet, 4$^1/_2$ inches in 1991?

 When Roger Maris hit his 61st home run in 1961, he broke Babe Ruth's legendary single-season record. Whose record did Ruth break when he hit his 60th home run in 1927?

 Who holds the major league record for career hits by a left-handed batter?

 What Dallas Cowboy set an NFL record with a 99-yard run from scrimmage on January 3, 1983?

 What Los Angeles Rams quarterback threw for a second 554 yards in one game in 1951?

 Which New York Yankee holds the World Series record for most career home runs: Babe Ruth, Reggie Jackson, or Mickey Mantle?

 Which New York Yankee holds the World Series record for most career hits: Yogi Berra, Lou Gehrig, or Joe DiMaggio?

 What Yankees pitcher holds the World Series record for career wins with 10?

 What former Heisman Trophy winner scored an NFL-record 176 points in 1960?

 What Los Angeles Laker once set an NBA record with 284 total points in a seven-game championship series?

Surprisingly, what franchise holds the American League record for wins in one season?

 What NFL record does Paul Krause hold?

 Despite holding the NFL's all-time passing yardage record, this quarterback never won a Super Bowl. Name him.

 In 1992, who set a world record in the decathlon, Dan or Dave?

 Tiger Williams averaged nearly 20 goals per season during his NHL career, but in what "offensive" category does he hold the league's all-time record?

## T I M E (00:00) T R I A L

Listed below in the column on the left are 10 of baseball's most famous record-holders. How quickly can you match them to the appropriate statistic from the center column and the year in which they set that record from the column on the right? In this event, your target time is 1:30, with the usual five-second penalty for each incorrect pairing.

| Hank Aaron | 4,192 | 1941 |
| Roger Clemens | 715 | 1961 |
| Joe DiMaggio | 383 | 1973 |
| Rickey Henderson | 130 | 1974 |
| Orel Hershiser | 61 | 1982 |
| Roger Maris | 59 | 1985 |
| Mark McGwire | 57 | 1986 |
| Peter Rose | 56 | 1987 |
| Nolan Ryan | 49 | 1988 |
| Bobby Thigpen | 20 | 1990 |

**Answers:** Hank Aaron (715 home runs, 1974), Roger Clemens (20 strikeouts in one game, 1986), Joe DiMaggio (56-game hitting streak, 1941), Rickey Henderson (130 stolen bases in one season, 1982), Orel Hershiser (59 consecutive scoreless innings, 1988), Roger Maris (61 home runs in one season, 1961), Mark McGwire (49 home runs in rookie season, 1987), Pete Rose (4,192 career hits, 1985), Nolan Ryan (383 strikeouts in one season, 1973), Bobby Thigpen (57 saves in one season, 1990)

In 1920, the St. Louis Browns' George Sisler set a major league batting record that still stands today. What record does Sisler hold?

 In 1930, what Chicago Cubs slugger set a major league record with 190 runs batted in?

 What NHL Hall of Famer won a record eight consecutive Norris Trophies from 1968 to 1975?

 Who holds the NHL record for goals in one season by a defenseman?

 Entering the 1994 season, the American League and National League save records were each held by pitchers from Chicago. Name them.

 Who holds the NBA record for scoring average by a rookie?

 Dale Long and Don Mattingly are two of only three players to hit home runs in eight consecutive games. Who tied their record in 1993?

 On September 7, 1993, who tied the major league record with 12 RBIs in one game?

 What Hall of Fame receiver holds the NFL record for most career scoring titles?

 What Hall of Fame slugger holds the major league record for career grand slams?

 On his way to winning the National League Cy Young Award, what pitcher appeared in a record 106 games in 1974?

 What NBA team set the all-time record for futility by going 9–73 during the 1972–73 season?

 What Philadelphia Flyer served an NHL-record 472 penalty minutes during the 1974–75 season?

Reggie Jackson is one of only two players to hit three home runs in one World Series game. Who was the other?

 In 1983, who set an NFL record with 24 rushing touchdowns?

 Everyone knows that Hank Aaron is the major league home-run king, but who holds the major league record for most career runs batted in?

 Of Aaron's record 755 home runs, 398 came as a member of the Milwaukee Braves. Who holds the Milwaukee Braves' career home-run record?

 During the 1993 season, who set an NFL record with five touchdowns in one playoff game?

 What Raiders linebacker set an NFL record with three interceptions in Super Bowl XV?

 On February 7, 1976, what Toronto Maple Leaf set an NHL record with 10 points in one game against the Boston Bruins?

 In men's track and field, which throwing event features the longest world record?

 When the Los Angeles Lakers set an NBA record with 33 consecutive wins in 1972, who broke their epic streak?

 At the start of the 1994 season, three NFL players shared the Super Bowl record for career points with 24. Name the only non-49er to accomplish that feat.

 Who holds the major league record for most consecutive scoreless innings pitched?

 What NHL goalie holds the record for most career shutouts?

 What quarterback holds the NFL record with 48 touchdown passes in a single season?

In baseball, what brother combination holds the major league record for most career victories?

 What current National League manager holds the all-time record for being hit by pitches?

 What Montreal Expo was hit by a major-league-record 50 pitches in 1971?

 What quarterback completed a record 88 percent of his pass attempts in Super Bowl XXI?

 What Dodgers pitcher holds the club record for career wins with 233?

 Who holds the New York Yankees' record for most games played?

 Name one of the two baseball Hall of Famers who share the record for All-Star Game appearances with 24.

# EXTRA POINT

What sporting event did Lee Haney win a record-setting eight times?

# CHALLENGE 6.

## NUMBERS UP

FROM WILT CHAMBERLAIN'S 100-POINT GAME TO ROGER MARIS'S 61 HOME RUNS, NUMBERS ARE A VITAL PART OF EVERY SPORTS FAN'S VOCABULARY, SO IN THIS CHAPTER, WE'VE COMPILED 50 QUESTIONS ABOUT SOME OF SPORTS' MOST FAMOUS FIGURES. IF YOU FAIL TO ANSWER 25 OF THEM, YOUR NUMBER IS UP, BUT IF YOU CAN CONNECT ON 35 OF 50, YOU SHOULD BREAK INTO THE TOP 20. FORTY-FIVE RIGHT ANSWERS WILL EARN YOU A PLACE IN THE FINAL FOUR, AND A PERFECT SCORE WILL MAKE YOU A UNANIMOUS CHOICE AS NUMBER ONE. AN-SWERS BEGIN ON PAGE 106.

One of baseball's most famous records is Lou Gehrig's streak of 2,130 consecutive games played. How many seasons did Gehrig's epic streak span?

 Entering the 1994 season, how many times has a Notre Dame player won college football's Heisman Trophy?

 How many schools play football in the Big 10?

 In thoroughbred racing, how many pounds must each horse carry during Triple Crown races?

 How many teams qualify for postseason play in the National Hockey League?

 New York Yankees managers Casey Stengel and Joe McCarthy share the major league record for World Series championships. How many World Series did each man win?

 How many All-Star Games did Ty Cobb play in?

 What uniform number did New York Yankees Hall of Famers Bill Dickey and Yogi Berra share?

 Statistically speaking, what famous number is shared by Mel Ott and Cy Young?

 If the home team loses, how many outs are there in a complete nine-inning baseball game?

 How many sides does home plate have?

 What is the official final score of a forfeited baseball game?

 What is the official final score of a forfeited football game?

 How many different positions did Pete Rose play in All-Star competition?

What uniform number did Joe Montana wear at Notre Dame?

 In the Ryder Cup competition, how many golfers make up each team?

 According to NFL rules, what is the highest number a kicker can wear on his jersey?

 As of 1994, how many teams qualify for postseason play in the NFL?

# T I M E 00:00 T R I A L

In the column on the left are the names of 15 prominent sports figures listed in alphabetical order. How quickly can you put them in numerical order by matching them to the appropriate uniform numbers in the column on the right? Once again, your target time is one minute, with a five-second penalty for each one you get wrong.

| | |
|---|---|
| Hank Aaron | 1 |
| Elgin Baylor | 3 |
| Larry Bird | 4 |
| Joe DiMaggio | 5 |
| Wayne Gretzky | 9 |
| Bob Griese | 12 |
| Bobby Hull | 20 |
| Magic Johnson | 22 |
| Michael Jordan | 23 |
| Billy Martin | 32 |
| Bobby Orr | 33 |
| Richard Petty | 37 |
| Babe Ruth | 43 |
| Mike Schmidt | 44 |
| Casey Stengel | 99 |

**Answers:** Martin (1), Ruth (3), Orr (4), DiMaggio (5), Hull (9), Griese (12), Schmidt (20), Baylor (22), Jordan (23), Johnson (32), Bird (33), Stengel (37), Petty (37), Aaron (44), Gretzky (99)

The number 63 is the only uniform number that has been retired by the Tampa Bay Buccaneers. Who wore it?

 Cuba's Javier Sotomayor was the first man ever to clear what landmark height in the high jump?

 How many gold medals did speed skater Eric Heiden win at the 1980 Winter Olympics?

 In pocket billiards, how many striped balls are used in a game of "nine-ball"?

 In women's track and field, how many events make up the heptathlon?

 In the poem "Casey at the Bat," what was the approximate attendance at the game?

 How long is a regulation soccer match?

 In addition to his nine Emmy Awards, how many Super Bowl rings did John Madden win?

 Within one pound, how heavy is the "hammer" in the hammer throw?

 Under normal conditions, how many laps does it take to win the Indianapolis 500?

 How many men's singles titles did Bjorn Borg win at Wimbledon?

 In minutes, how long is a twelve-round boxing match?

 In the 1985–86 regular season, the Boston Celtics posted the best home record in NBA history. How many home games did they lose that season?

 An NBA basketball court is 94 feet long. Within two feet, how wide is it?

In major league history, only two pitchers have recorded 4,000 career strikeouts. Name them.

 How many different times did Billy Martin manage the New York Yankees?

 Though O. J. Simpson is now famous for wearing number 32, what Buffalo Bill wore that number during O. J. Simpson's rookie season with the team?

 Early Wynn is one of only two pitchers to retire with exactly 300 wins. Who was the other?

 Besides O. J. Simpson, name the only other NFL player to rush for more than 2,000 yards in one season.

 Name the only major league player in the twentieth century to finish his career with exactly 3,000 hits.

 In terms of seating capacity, the smallest arena in the NBA holds only 12,888 people. Which arena is it?

 After boldly guaranteeing a New York Jets victory, Joe Namath was named Most Valuable Player in Super Bowl III. How many touchdown passes did Namath throw that day?

 What is par at the legendary Pebble Beach Golf Links?

 In baseball's All-Star Game, how many innings is a starting pitcher allowed to pitch?

 Which league's teams play more regular-season games, the NHL or the NBA?

 The number 6 is the only uniform number ever retired by the San Diego Padres. Who wore it?

 In the direct center, how high is a regulation tennis net?

 In baseball, what percentage of the votes must a Coopers-

**challenge 6.**

town candidate receive in order to gain induction to the Hall of Fame?

 In basketball, how far is it from the basket to the free-throw line?

 In a perfect game of bowling, how many strikes are rolled?

 In horse racing, how long is a furlong?

What landmark barrier did pole vaulter Sergei Bubka break in 1991?

EXTRA POINT

At New York's Madison Square Garden, what number hangs from the rafters in honor of former Knicks coach Red Holzman?

# CHALLENGE 7.

# THE NAME GAME

NOW THAT WE'VE REVIEWED OUR NUMBERS, LET'S FIND OUT HOW WELL YOU KNOW YOUR ABC'S. FROM THE GAS HOUSE GANG TO THE BIG RED MACHINE, COLORFUL NICKNAMES ARE A PROMINENT PART OF SPORTS HISTORY, AND IN THIS CHAPTER, THEY PLAY A PROMINENT ROLE IN ALL 50 QUESTIONS. IF YOU CAN'T ANSWER 25 OF THEM, YOUR NAME MIGHT AS WELL BE "MUD," BUT IF YOU KNOW 45 OUT OF 50, "CHAMP" WOULD BE MORE APPROPRIATE. ANYONE WHO GETS ALL 50 CAN CALL THEMSELVES WHATEVER THEY WANT. ANSWERS BEGIN ON PAGE 110.

The Colorado Rockies and the Florida Marlins are the only National League teams named after states instead of cities. Name the three American League clubs that do not have a city in their team name.

 Which three major league baseball teams are named after birds?

 The 1927 New York Yankees were one of the most dangerous offensive teams in major league history. What was their lineup's colorful nickname?

 What Detroit Tiger was known as "The Bird"?

 What New York Giants pitcher was nicknamed "The Meal Ticket"?

 One of the two most popular nicknames in college sports is also the nickname of an American League team. What is it?

 In 1982, the SMU Mustangs featured a pair of 1,000-yard rushers nicknamed "The Pony Express." Who were they?

 The 1941 Heisman Trophy winner and the NFL's top draft pick in 1985 share the same name. What is it?

 In what year did the Super Bowl officially become "The Super Bowl"?

 What Washington Redskins running back was known as "The Diesel"?

 The last two-way player in the NFL was nicknamed "Concrete Charlie." What was his real name?

 In the 1970s, what NFL team's offensive line was known as "The Electric Company"?

 When the 1972 Miami Dolphins finished the season undefeated, their defense made quite a name for itself. What was it?

 What NFL Hall of Famer was nicknamed "Sweetness"?

 What was the original name of the Kansas City Chiefs?

 What legendary running back was nicknamed "The Galloping Ghost"?

# T I M E 00:00 T R I A L

In this event, see how quickly you can match the sports figures in the column on the left to the appropriate nickname in the column on the right. All the nicknames contain the word "big," and if you finish in under one minute, consider yourself "big time." Remember, though, there's a big five-second penalty for each one you get wrong.

| | |
|---|---|
| Anaheim Stadium | Big Cat |
| Wilt Chamberlain | Big Dog |
| Don Drysdale | Big Hurt |
| Clarence Gaines | Big Train |
| Don Garlits | Big House |
| Elvin Hayes | Big Daddy |
| Walter Johnson | Big Poison |
| Frank Mahovolich | Big Six |
| Man O' War | Big Red |
| Christy Mathewson | Big Dipper |
| Johnny Mize | Big A |
| Oscar Robertson | Big D |
| Glenn Robinson | Big E |
| Frank Thomas | Big M |
| Paul Waner | Big O |

**Answers:** Anaheim Stadium (The Big A), Wilt Chamberlain (The Big Dipper), Don Drysdale (Big D), Clarence Gaines (Big House), Don Garlits (Big Daddy), Elvin Hayes (The Big E), Walter Johnson (The Big Train), Frank Mahovolich (The Big M), Man O' War (Big Red), Christy Mathewson (Big Six), Johnny Mize (The Big Cat), Oscar Robertson (The Big O), Glenn Robinson (The Big Dog), Frank Thomas (The Big Hurt), Paul Waner (Big Poison)

**17** In the 1950 NFL Championship Game, Lou Groza's last-minute field goal gave the Cleveland Browns a 30–28 victory over the Los Angeles Rams. What was Groza's apt nickname?

**18** What All-Pro linebacker earned his nickname by cutting a car in half while at the University of Tennessee?

**19** What NFL quarterback was known as "The Snake"?

**20** Nicknamed "Night Train," this defensive back set an NFL record with 14 interceptions for the Detroit Lions in 1952. Name him.

**21** Which four NFL football teams are named after birds?

**22** What was the nickname of NFL Hall of Famer Elroy Hirsch?

**23** In Super Bowl XV, one of the starting quarterbacks was nicknamed "The Polish Rifle." Who was he?

**24** Before switching to a more geographic alignment in 1993, what were the names of the four NHL divisions?

**25** Nicknamed "Boom Boom," this former Montreal Canadiens star was also the first coach of the old Atlanta Flames. Name him.

**26** Nicknamed "The Flying Finn," this runner won nine gold medals during his Olympic career. What was his real name?

**27** What is legendary pool shark Rudolf Wanderone better known as?

**28** When the Carolina Panthers join the NFL in 1995, they will share a nickname with the NHL's Florida Panthers. Name the two other nicknames that are shared by NHL and NFL teams.

**29** In the NHL and NBA, a pair of California teams are the only ones to share a nickname. Name them.

What legendary baseball manager was nicknamed "The Lip"?

 The Boston Red Sox and Chicago White Sox are the only major league baseball teams whose nicknames do not end with the letter s. Can you name the three NBA teams whose names do not end in s?

 Name the only NHL team whose nickname does not end with the letter s.

 In track and field, "Flo-Jo" has an equally famous sister-in-law. Name her.

 In the NHL, who was "The Golden Jet"?

 What National League team was known as "The Gas House Gang"?

 What is pro football's Bobby Moore better known as?

 What was the nickname of tennis great René Lacoste?

 What sport did seven-footer André René Roussimof excel at?

 What boxer was known as "The Louisville Lip"?

 In the movie *Rocky*, who wins the big fight?

 In auto racing, where would one find "The Brickyard"?

 In golf, what was the nickname of Arnold Palmer's loyal gallery?

 What sport features a 560-pound competitor nicknamed "Meat Bomb"?

 What NFL team once featured a trio of speedy receivers known as "The Three Amigos"?

 When the Cincinnati Reds won the World Series in 1990, what was the nickname of their hard-throwing bullpen?

the name game

By what name is Edson Arantes do Nascimento better known?

 What is the real first name of Hall of Fame pitcher "Satchel" Paige?

 What baseball movie featured a character named Crash Davis?

 In what major sporting event do the finals take place at Louis Armstrong Stadium?

What was the Denver Nuggets' Mahmoud Abdul-Raul known as when he played at Louisiana State?

# EXTRA POINT

In 1969, what major sports league was composed of the Capital, Century, Central, and Coastal divisions?

# CHALLENGE 8.

# CHAMPS AND CHUMPS

IN SPORTS, IT'S AXIOMATIC THAT FOR EVERY WINNER THERE MUST ALSO BE A LOSER, AND FOR EVERY HERO THERE IS USUALLY A CORRESPONDING GOAT. IN THIS CHAPTER, ALL 50 QUESTIONS ARE DEDICATED TO THOSE ATHLETES AND TEAMS WHO LEFT THEIR MARK ON HISTORY, EITHER BY ALWAYS COMING THROUGH OR FOREVER COMING UP SHORT. IF YOU CAN'T ANSWER 25 OF THESE QUESTIONS, CONSIDER YOURSELF IN THE LATTER CLASS, BUT IF YOU GUESS RIGHT ON 35 OF 50, YOU'RE ON YOUR WAY TO A WINNING SEASON. FORTY-FIVE RIGHT PUTS YOU IN THE WORLD SERIES,

AND IF YOU NAIL ALL 50, PERHAPS YOU SHOULD CHANGE YOUR NAME TO MAZEROSKI. IF YOU DON'T UNDERSTAND THAT LAST REFERENCE, YOU PROBABLY WON'T NEED TO, BUT YOU WILL NEED TO CHECK OUT THE ANSWERS, WHICH BEGIN ON PAGE 114.

1. Despite batting .408 in 1911 and .356 during his 13-year career, this notorious slugger never won a batting title. Who is he?

2. When Nolan Ryan joined baseball's 3,000-strikeout club on July 4, 1980, his 3,000th victim was the same as Bob Gibson's six years earlier. Name him.

3. Name the only member of baseball's 500-home run club never to play in the World Series.

4. Besides the Colorado Rockies and the Florida Marlins, name the two other National League teams that have never reached the World Series.

5. Name the only three American League teams never to play in a World Series.

6. On July 24, 1993, what New York Mets pitcher set a major league record with his 27th consecutive loss?

7. When Don Larsen pitched his perfect game in the 1956 World Series, who was the losing pitcher?

8. In 1968, what golfer forfeited the Masters championship when he signed his scorecard incorrectly?

9. At the 1993 PGA Championship, what golfer became only the second man ever to lose all four of the Grand Slam events in a playoff?

10. Which four AFC teams have never played in the Super Bowl?

**58**

Which five NFC teams have never played in the Super Bowl?

 Who was the losing quarterback in Super Bowl I and the MVP in Super Bowl IV?

 In Miami's 14–7 victory over Washington in Super Bowl VII, who threw the pass that gave the Redskins their only touchdown?

 In Super Bowl XIII, what Hall of Fame tight end dropped a sure touchdown pass in the third quarter, possibly costing the Dallas Cowboys a victory over the Pittsburgh Steelers?

# T I M E (00:00) T R I A L

Listed below in the column on the left are players who hit 10 of the most famous home runs in baseball history. How quickly can you match them to their somewhat less-famous victims. As usual, your target time is one minute, with a five-second penalty for each pitcher you wrongly identify.

| | |
|---|---|
| Hank Aaron | Ralph Branca |
| Joe Carter | Pat Darcy |
| Chris Chambliss | Al Downing |
| Carlton Fisk | Dennis Eckersley |
| Kirk Gibson | Mark Littell |
| Roger Maris | Charlie Root |
| Bill Mazeroski | Rip Sewell |
| Babe Ruth | Tracy Stallard |
| Bobby Thomson | Ralph Terry |
| Ted Williams | Mitch Williams |

**Answers:** Hank Aaron and Al Downing (Aaron's 715th home run), Joe Carter and Mitch Williams (1993 World Series), Chris Chambliss and Mark Littell (1976 American League Championship Series), Carlton Fisk and Pat Darcy (1975 World Series), Kirk Gibson and Dennis Eckersley (1988 World Series), Roger Maris and Tracy Stallard (Maris's 61st home run in 1961), Bill Mazeroski and Ralph Terry (1960 World Series), Babe Ruth and Charlie Root (1932 World Series), Bobby Thomson and Ralph Branca (1951 National League playoff), Ted Williams and Rip Sewell (1946 All-Star Game)

In yachting, who was the first American skipper to lose the America's Cup?

 Despite winning the second-highest number of Grand Slam singles championships in men's tennis history, there are two Grand Slam events that Bjorn Borg never won. Name them.

 Name the only Grand Slam singles title that Ivan Lendl has never won.

 What team always loses to the Harlem Globetrotters?

 Name the only manager to win a World Series championship in both the American and National leagues.

 Who is the only golfer to win an event on the regular PGA Tour and the Senior Tour in the same year?

 What NFL team has appeared in the Super Bowl the most times?

 Name the only "wild-card" team to win a Super Bowl.

 Who is the only football player to play in the Rose Bowl, the Super Bowl, and the Grey Cup (the Canadian Football League championship game)?

 How many times did Bill Walsh lead the San Francisco 49ers to the Super Bowl title?

 Name the only coach to win both a Super Bowl and a college football national championship.

 Name the only coach to win both an NBA championship and an Olympic gold medal.

 Whose touchdown reception with 39 seconds left in the game gave the San Francisco 49ers a 20–16 win over the Cincinnati Bengals in Super Bowl XXIII?

 Who rode Secretariat to the Triple Crown in 1973?

In the NHL, the Montreal Canadiens have won the most Stanley Cups with 24. Which team has won the second-most Cups?

 What country did the United States defeat to win the gold medal in ice hockey at the 1980 Winter Olympics?

 Only two of boxing's world heavyweight champions have also been heavyweight gold-medal winners at the Olympics. Name them.

 What country did George Best lead to the World Cup title in 1966?

 In tennis, who won the U.S. Open in 1979 at the tender age of 16?

 What boxer won the world heavyweight championship by upsetting Muhammad Ali on February 15, 1978?

 Name the only world heavyweight champion to retire undefeated.

 What team has made the most appearances in the NBA finals?

 What Canadian sprinter was stripped of both his gold medal and his world record at the 1988 Summer Olympics?

 Who was the first woman to cross the finish line in the 1980 Boston Marathon?

 In the 1954 World Series, Willie Mays made what many fans feel is the greatest catch in baseball history. Who was the unlucky batter who hit the ball that Mays caught?

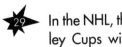 After player strikes interrupted the 1982 and 1987 NFL seasons, the same team went on to win the Super Bowl each time. Name it.

**challenge 8.**

 **41** In baseball, which franchise has lost the World Series the most times?

 **42** The team that won the last ABA championship in 1976 is now a member of the NBA. Name it.

 **43** On May 26, 1959, what frustrated pitcher threw a perfect game for 12 innings but still lost the game in the 13th?

 **44** In 1993, the San Francisco Giants failed to reach the play-offs despite winning 103 games. Name the last American League team to win 100 games and still miss the playoffs.

 **45** What player was named MVP of the first two Super Bowls?

 **46** What British sprinter won the gold medal in the men's 100-meter dash at the 1992 Barcelona Olympics?

 **47** What Kenyan runner upset Jim Ryun to win the gold medal in the 1,500 meters at the 1968 Summer Olympics?

 **48** The 1984 Olympic gold medalist in men's figure skating was also the world champion for four straight years. Name him.

 **49** In boxing, who was the last bare-knuckle champion of the world?

 **50** In 1985, who became the youngest player ever to win a men's singles championship at Wimbledon?

# EXTRA POINT

In thoroughbred racing, only one "father-and-son" combination have each won the Triple Crown. Who were they?

62

# AND THE WINNER IS . . .

FOR ATHLETES, WINNING A CHAMPIONSHIP IS ALWAYS THE ULTIMATE GOAL, BUT WINNING AN INDIVIDUAL AWARD USUALLY PLACES A CLOSE SECOND. IN THIS CHAPTER, ALL 50 QUESTIONS INVOLVE PLAYERS WHO WERE OUTSTANDING IN THEIR FIELDS AND BROUGHT HOME THE HARDWARE TO PROVE IT. IF YOU CAN'T ANSWER 25, YOU WON'T BE WINNING ANY AWARDS, BUT 35 OUT OF 50 WILL EARN YOU A FEW WRITE-IN VOTES. FORTY-FIVE RIGHT ANSWERS MAKES YOU AN MVP CANDIDATE, AND WITH A PERFECT SCORE YOU CAN BOOK YOUR RESERVATIONS FOR THE HALL OF FAME. ANSWERS BEGIN ON PAGE 119.

Who is the only pitcher to win the Cy Young Award in each league?

 What third baseman won a major league 16 Gold Gloves?

 In 1992, who became the only player in major league history to win a home-run title in both leagues?

 What shortstop holds the National League record for most career Gold Gloves?

 In 1960, this Yankees second baseman became the only player ever to be named World Series MVP despite playing for the losing team. Name him.

 Who is the only player to win the American League Most Valuable Player Award in both the 1980s and the 1990s?

 In 1979, which two players shared the National League MVP award?

 In 1985, what American League slugger became the oldest player ever to win a home-run title?

 Frank Robinson is the only baseball player to be named MVP in each league. With which team did he win the Triple Crown in 1966?

 After capturing the Heisman Trophy in 1980, this Gamecock went on to become the NFL rushing champion in 1981. Name him.

 What Cowboy is the only player to be named Super Bowl MVP in a losing cause?

 What New York Giant was named game MVP when his team defeated the Buffalo Bills in Super Bowl XXV?

Name the only Super Bowl MVP to later become a head coach in the NFL.

 In 1980, this player became the last man besides Wayne Gretzky and Mario Lemieux to win the NHL scoring title. Name him.

 What Philadelphia Flyer won three NHL MVP Awards during the 1970s?

 Who was the only player from a losing team to be named MVP of the NBA finals?

 Wilt Chamberlain is one of only two players to be named NBA MVP in his rookie season. Who was the other?

 Who is the only basketball player to be named league Most Valuable Player in both the ABA and the NBA?

# T I M E 00:00 T R I A L

Match the following trophies and awards to the sports that confer them. As usual, your target time is one minute, with a five-second penalty for each incorrect answer.

| | |
|---|---|
| Eclipse Award | Auto Racing |
| Federation Cup | Baseball |
| Harlon Hill Trophy | Basketball (college) |
| James Naismith Award | Basketball (professional) |
| Maurice Podoloff Trophy | Football |
| Rolaids Trophy | Golf (Men's) |
| Solheim Cup | Golf (Women's) |
| Vardon Trophy | Hockey |
| Vezina Trophy | Horse Racing |
| Borg Warner Trophy | Tennis |

**Answers:** *Eclipse Award (horse racing), Federation Cup (tennis), Harlon Hill Trophy (college football), James Naismith Award (college basketball), Maurice Podoloff Trophy (professional basketball), Rolaids Trophy (baseball), Solheim Cup (women's golf), Vardon Trophy (men's golf), Vezina Trophy (hockey), Borg Warner Trophy (auto racing)*

During the 1980s, the Philadelphia 76ers, Boston Celtics, Los Angeles Lakers, and Detroit Pistons were the only teams to win NBA championships. Can you name the only player to win three straight MVP Awards during that decade?

 Moses Malone is one of only two NBA players to win the league MVP Award with two different teams. Who is the other?

 If you were the most sportsmanlike player in the NHL, what award would you receive?

 In the NHL, who is eligible to win the Calder Trophy?

 When Ted Williams batted .406 in 1941, somebody else was named American League MVP. Who was it?

 What female sprinter won four gold medals at the 1988 Summer Olympics?

 What young tennis player upset Steffi Graf to win the gold medal at the 1992 Barcelona Olympics?

 What Cuban heavyweight won three straight Olympic gold medals in boxing?

 What U.S. swimmer won seven medals at the 1988 Summer Olympics?

 Name one of the two drivers to win both an Indianapolis 500 and a Daytona 500.

 From 1978 to 1988, this Norwegian runner won the New York Marathon a record nine times. Name her.

 What runner won three consecutive Boston Marathons from 1978 to 1980?

 Name the only tennis player to win four consecutive men's singles titles at the French Open.

Who is the only male tennis player to win the Grand Slam twice?

 What woman won four consecutive U.S. Open singles titles from 1975 to 1978?

 During the 1980s, what British runner won two Olympic gold medals in the 1500 meters?

 From 1979 through 1982, the same team produced the National League Rookie of the Year each season. Which team was it?

 Who is the only player to win the Cy Young Award while pitching for two different teams in the same season?

 Name the only pitcher to win back-to-back Most Valuable Player Awards.

 Who is the only player to win three Super Bowl MVP Awards?

 Who was the first defenseman to win the NHL scoring title?

 At the 1984 Summer Olympics, Carl Lewis won gold medals in the same four events that Jesse Owens did in 1936. Name them.

 In 1980, who became the youngest player ever to win the Masters?

 In 1955, what American Leaguer became the youngest player ever to win a batting championship?

 What slugging third baseman won eight National League home-run titles?

Name the only California Angel to win an American League batting title.

45 What Washington Redskin won six NFL passing titles and four NFL punting titles?

 46 Besides 1994 champ David Robinson, name the only other active player to win an NBA scoring title.

 47 Name the only player to win the NBA scoring and assist titles in the same season.

 48 What former UCLA center was the only player to lead both the NBA and ABA in rebounding?

 49 Name the only player to win the scoring title in both the NBA and the ABA.

 50 Since the Heisman Trophy was first awarded in 1935, the University of Alabama has won seven college football national championships. How many Heisman Trophy winners has the school produced?

EXTRA POINT

Which three Heisman Trophy winners have also been named Super Bowl MVPs?

# CHALLENGE 10.

## GRAB BAG

THROUGHOUT THIS BOOK, WE'VE TRIED TO MEASURE THE DEPTH OF YOUR SPORTS KNOWLEDGE BY ASKING QUESTIONS THAT TOUCH *ALL* THE BASES, FROM NINETEENTH-CENTURY BOXING TO THE MODERN PENTATHLON. IN THIS CHAPTER, HOWEVER, WE'VE SAVED THE BEST FOR LAST—A MOUNTAIN OF MISCELLANY THAT CONTAINS 50 QUESTIONS WITH NOTHING AT ALL IN COMMON, EXCEPT FOR THE FACT THAT THEY DIDN'T SEEM TO FIT ANYWHERE ELSE. ON THIS FINAL EXAM, A SCORE OF 25 OR LESS MEANS YOU SHOULD PROBABLY START OVER WITH CHALLENGE 1, WHILE 35 OUT OF 50 WILL

EARN YOU A PASSING MARK. FORTY-FIVE RIGHT ANSWERS WILL GET YOU A PLACE ON THE HONOR ROLL, AND A PERFECT 50 MEANS YOU SHOULD PROBABLY BE TEACHING THIS CLASS YOURSELF (HAVE YOU EVER THOUGHT OF WRITING YOUR OWN SPORTS-TRIVIA BOOK?). ANSWERS BEGIN ON PAGE 124.

 What minor league baseball team was championed by Corporal Klinger on the television series *M*A*S*H*?

 What color is the ejection card in soccer?

 What sport is featured in the film *Endless Summer*?

 What drink is traditionally associated with the Kentucky Derby?

 What unit of measurement is used to size horses?

 Name the only person who is a member of the college football, pro football, and baseball Halls of Fame.

 Where are track and field's Millrose Games held?

 In what country will you find the world's oldest golf course?

 Which baseball stadium is older, Chicago's Wrigley Field or Detroit's Tiger Stadium?

 Which NFL stadium has the smallest seating capacity?

 Of the boxing weight classes lightweight, flyweight, bantamweight, and featherweight, which one is the lightest?

 Name either one of the two major league players who have recorded a 200-hit season in each league.

# TIME [00:00] TRIAL

With a target time of 1:30, our final trial is a chance for you to make up some serious ground. Simply decide if each of the following 10 statements is true or false, and remember to penalize yourself five seconds for each one you get wrong. A total time of 12 minutes for all 10 trials is what you need to bring home the gold medal (13:30 will get you silver, and 15:00 is good for bronze), so after you figure out how fast you need to complete your final event, get to it!

A regulation Frisbee is twelve inches in diameter.

Bernard King is the only New York Knick to lead the NBA in scoring.

The five rings on an archery target are the same colors as the Olympic rings.

In the year 2000, the Summer Olympics will be held in Athens, Greece.

On a golf scoreboard, sub-par scores are indicated in red.

The Brooklyn Dodgers never won the World Series.

The person who steers a bobsled is called "the driver."

In pocket billiards, the nine ball is white with a red stripe.

No American League player has ever won three consecutive MVP Awards.

On a dartboard, the number 20 falls between the numbers 1 and 5.

What is the height of an NFL crossbar?

 In addition to sharing part of their names, the 1975 American League MVP and the 1976 Super Bowl MVP were once roommates at USC. Name them.

 During World War II, what two cities were home to an NFL team called the "Steagles"?

 Name the only current NFL team that regularly plays its home games at two different stadiums.

 Name the only NFL team that plays its home games in New York State.

 In what state would you find the Cactus League?

 In baseball, what brother combo hit the most career home runs?

 What two brothers played for the 1980 American League champion Kansas City Royals?

 What Olympic filmmaker produced and directed the classic *16 Days to Glory*?

 What company is the sole manufacturer of major league baseballs?

 During the NHL playoffs, which team's fans traditionally throw an octopus onto the ice?

 What former Oriole is the only pitcher to hit a grand slam in the World Series?

 In what sport could you use a pen grip to hold your sandwich bat?

Within one, what is the maximum number of characters in a registered thoroughbred's name?

27 ▸ In baseball, only two players have been inducted into the Hall of Fame before the mandatory five-year waiting period expired. Name them.

28 ▸ Who is the youngest player ever to be inducted into baseball's Hall of Fame?

29 ▸ Who played Babe Ruth in the film *Pride of the Yankees*?

30 ▸ Super Bowl VIII is the only Super Bowl to be played in the state of Texas. What stadium was the game played in?

31 ▸ Of the three stadiums that have hosted both a World Series and a Super Bowl, only one is not in California. Name it.

32 ▸ During the 1944 World Series, what Midwest stadium hosted all six games?

33 ▸ What was the site of the only Olympics to take place in the Southern Hemisphere?

34 ▸ What bicoastal slugger was both the youngest and oldest player ever to hit 50 home runs in one season?

35 ▸ Name the only major league player to win a batting title in three different decades.

36 ▸ What future President was MVP of the 1934 Michigan football team?

37 ▸ What future President captained Yale's baseball team in 1948?

38 ▸ Pete Rose only hit one grand slam during his 24-year career, and it came off one of his future managers. Name him.

39 ▸ On a dogleg right, should a left-handed golfer play a draw or a fade?

40 ▸ What golfer reached the LPGA Hall of Fame at age 30, just 10 years after being named Rookie of the Year in 1977?

Who is the only player in major league history to hit for the cycle in each league?

 Name the only player in NFL history to run for 90 or more yards on one play twice in his career.

 Entering the 1994 season, name the only two left-handed quarterbacks to start in a Super Bowl.

 In thoroughbred racing's Triple Crown, which race is the shortest?

 The site of the 1972 Winter Olympics was scheduled to host the games in 1940 as well, but they were canceled due to World War II. Name this Asian city.

 Besides Lake Placid, New York, name the only other American city to host the Winter Olympics.

 In what event did World War II hero George Patton compete at the 1912 Olympics?

 What sport features a bowler, a batsman, and a wicket-keeper?

 When Wilt Chamberlain scored 100 points against the New York Knicks on March 2, 1962, where was the game played?

 What sport was featured in the 1972 Raquel Welch movie *Kansas City Bombers*?

# EXTRA POINT

In the Abbott and Costello routine "Who's on First?," what team do the players play for?

# T HE ANSWERS

*Ted Williams. In 1941, Williams batted .406 for the Boston Red Sox.*

*Archie Griffin. At Ohio State, Griffin won the award as a junior in 1974 and again as a senior in 1975.*

*The Big 10 and the Pac-10.*

*The Detroit Red Wings, Chicago Blackhawks, Boston Bruins, New York Rangers, Montreal Canadiens, and Toronto Maple Leafs.*

*Bobby Thomson. On October 3, 1951, Thomson's three-run home run in the bottom half of the ninth inning gave the New York Giants a 6–4 victory over the Brooklyn Dodgers and sent the Giants to the World Series.*

**75**

☞ 6 Secretariat.

☞ 7 The high jump. Fosbury revolutionized the sport by jumping over the bar backward, a maneuver that became known as "The Fosbury Flop."

☞ 8 The Boston Celtics. As of 1994, the Celtics had won 16 NBA titles, including eight in a row from 1959 to 1966.

☞ 9 The Chicago Cubs.

☞ 10 The Green Bay Packers and the Kansas City Chiefs. Green Bay won, 35–10.

☞ 11 Foil, sabre, and épée.

☞ 12 Roger Bannister. A medical student from England, Bannister broke the four-minute barrier with a 3:59.4 mile on May 6, 1954.

☞ 13 The Mudville Nine.

☞ 14 Muhammad Ali and Joe Frazier. Ali won on a TKO in the 15th round.

☞ 15 The Harlem Globetrotters.

☞ 16 Ice hockey. Awarded to the top college player each season, it is the equivalent of football's Heisman Trophy, and is named after a former Princeton University star who was killed during World War I.

☞ 17 Pete Maravich. In the 1969–70 season, "Pistol Pete" averaged an incredible 44.2 points per game for Louisiana State.

☞ 18 John Wooden. Nicknamed "The Wizard of Westwood," Wooden also led the Bruins to titles in 1964, 1965, and 1975.

☞ 19 Texas Western. In a landmark game, Texas Western used an all-black starting lineup to defeat Adolph Rupp's all-white Kentucky squad, 72–65, for the 1966 NCAA basketball championship.

☞ 20 The pitcher and the catcher.

☞ 21 Greg LeMond. LeMond actually won the event three times: 1986, 1989, and 1990.

22 Hit a single, a double, a triple, and a home run, all in the same game, a feat even rarer than a no-hitter.

23 The University of Chicago's Jay Berwanger, in 1935.

24 Kenesaw Mountain Landis. Landis was appointed in 1920 in the wake of the "Black Sox" World Series scandal, and served until his death in 1944.

25 Tom Dempsey. In 1970, Dempsey booted a 63-yarder as time expired to give the New Orleans Saints a 19–17 victory over the Detroit Lions.

26 Chicago Bears 73, Washington Redskins 0.

27 755.

28 Sadaharu Oh. Oh slugged his 756th career home run for Japan's Tokyo Giants on September 3, 1977, and finished his career with an amazing 868.

29 The Masters.

30 Mr. Inside and Mr. Outside. During the 1940s, they won back-to-back Heisman Trophies, with Blanchard winning in 1945 and Davis duplicating the feat in 1946.

31 Swimming, bicycling, and running, or more specifically, a 2.2-mile swim, a 112-mile bike ride, and a full 26.2-mile marathon.

32 Roger Maris, with 61 in 1961.

33 Wilt Chamberlain. On March 2, 1962, Chamberlain scored an amazing 100 points for the Philadelphia Warriors in a game against the New York Knicks.

34 He walked on four pitches. Gaedel was the midget whom St. Louis Browns owner Bill Veeck sent to bat as a publicity stunt on August 9, 1951.

35 Wimbledon, the French Open, the U.S. Open, and the Australian Open.

36 The Masters, the U.S. Open, the British Open, and the PGA Championship.

☞ 37 *In order, the three Triple Crown races are the Kentucky Derby, the Preakness Stakes, and the Belmont Stakes.*

☞ 38 *Batting average, home runs, and runs batted in.*

☞ 39 *Carl Yastrzemski, who hit .326 with 44 HR and 126 RBI for the Boston Red Sox in 1967.*

☞ 40 *Known as "The Father of Baseball," Doubleday was wrongly credited with inventing the game in Cooperstown, New York, in 1839. Despite the error, however, Cooperstown remains the site of baseball's Hall of Fame, and the annual Hall of Fame Game is played each summer at nearby Doubleday Field.*

☞ 41 *Dr. James Naismith. In 1891, Naismith invented the game as an indoor winter activity for his YMCA class in Springfield, Massachusetts.*

☞ 42 *The Marquis of Queensbury.*

☞ 43 *The five countries to win multiple World Cups are Italy (1934, 1938, and 1982), West Germany (1954, 1974, and 1990), Brazil (1958, 1962, 1970, and 1994), Argentina (1978 and 1986), and Uruguay (1930 and 1950).*

☞ 44 *Don Larsen. On October 8, 1956, Larsen pitched a perfect game for the New York Yankees, shutting out the Brooklyn Dodgers 2–0 in Game Five of the World Series. New York went on to win the series, four games to three.*

☞ 45 *Mark Spitz.*

☞ 46 *Maurice Richard. In the 1944–45 season, Richard scored 50 goals for the Montreal Canadiens, making him the only NHL player ever to score 50 goals in a 50-game season.*

☞ 47 *Joe DiMaggio. In 1941, "Joltin' Joe" hit safely in 56 consecutive games, 12 more than any other player in baseball history.*

☞ 48 *City College of New York. In 1950, when the tournaments were played at different times, CCNY defeated Bradley for both the NCAA championship and the NIT title.*

**78**

49 *Notre Dame. On their way to winning the national championship in 1924, it was the nickname given to the star backfield of Jim Crowley, Don Miller, Elmer Layden, and Harry Stuldreher.*

50 *The Los Angeles Rams. The name referred to the defensive line of Rosey Grier, Lamar Lundy, Deacon Jones, and Merlin Olsen.*

51 *Janet Guthrie. She broke the gender barrier by qualifying for the field of 33 in 1976.*

52 *Jack Dempsey and Gene Tunney.*

53 *At Fenway Park, home of the Boston Red Sox. The Green Monster, Fenway's left-field wall, is 37 feet, 6 inches high.*

54 *Playing for the University of California, Riegels ran the wrong way after recovering a fumble, giving the ball to Georgia Tech on the Cal one-yard line. Tech scored on the next play, and went on to win the game, 8–7.*

55 *Temple, Villanova, St. Joseph's, LaSalle, and Pennsylvania.*

56 *George Blanda. Blanda scored 2,002 points in his 26-year career.*

57 *Kareem Abdul-Jabbar. In 16 seasons with the Milwaukee Bucks and the Los Angeles Lakers, Kareem scored 38,387 points, an average of 24.6 per game.*

58 *Wayne Gretzky. During the 1993–94 season, Gretzky scored his 802nd career goal, surpassing the mark held by the legendary Gordie Howe.*

59 *Ty Cobb. From 1905 to 1928, Cobb scored 2,245 runs for the Detroit Tigers and the Philadelphia Athletics.*

60 *Pacing and trotting. In pacing, both legs on the same side of the horse move together, while in trotting, the front and rear legs on opposite sides of the horse move together.*

61 *Notre Dame. In January of that season, the Fighting Irish upended the Bruins, 71–70.*

62 *Pheidippides. During a battle in 490 B.C., he supposedly ran over twenty-five miles to deliver a message to his commander in the city of Marathon, then collapsed and died.*

63 *Herschel Walker and Doug Flutie. Walker won the Heisman as a running back for the University of Georgia in 1982, while Flutie won the award two years later as a quarterback for Boston College.*

64 *Cross-country skiing and shooting.*

65 *Bob Beamon. In the thin air of Mexico City, Beamon's gold-medal jump broke the previous mark by nearly two feet and stood as the world record for more than 20 years.*

66 *The New York Jets, 16–7, over the Baltimore Colts in Super Bowl III.*

67 *The Miami Dolphins. In 1972, the Dolphins finished the regular season 14–0, then went on to defeat the Washington Redskins in Super Bowl VII.*

68 *Billie Jean King and Bobby Riggs. In a special one-match showdown at the Houston Astrodome, King defeated Riggs, 6–4, 6–3, 6–3.*

69 *Akron, Ohio.*

70 *Three goals in one game by the same player.*

71 *The 1,500-meter run.*

72 *Jim Bouton.*

73 *Al Oerter of the United States.*

74 *Byron "Whizzer" White. As a running back at the University of Colorado, White finished second in the 1938 Heisman Trophy voting, but he played just three seasons in the NFL before embarking on a law career. He was appointed to the Supreme Court by John F. Kennedy in 1962.*

75 *Williamsport, Pennsylvania.*

76 *Alaska. The Iditarod is an annual sled-dog race that runs from Anchorage to Nome, a distance of 1,049 miles.*

(77) *A bottle of milk.*

(78) *Diego Maradona. After illegally batting the ball forward with his hand, Maradona scored the winning goal for Argentina, which went on to win the championship game as well.*

(79) *Boris Spassky.*

(80) *Sandy Koufax, with four.*

(81) *Mike Tyson. Tyson was just 20 years old when he knocked out Trevor Berbick on November 22, 1986.*

(82) *Tommie Smith and John Carlos. Smith and Carlos finished first and third, respectively, in the 200-meter run, but were suspended from the team after raising their fists in protest during the playing of the U.S. National Anthem.*

(83) *Besides Shoeless Joe, the other seven Black Sox were pitchers Lefty Williams and Ed Cicotte, first baseman Chick Gandil, shortstop Swede Risberg, third basemen Buck Weaver and Fred McMullin, and outfielder Hap Felsch. All eight were banned from baseball for life for their part in fixing the 1919 World Series, which the Chicago White Sox lost to the Cincinnati Reds, five games to three.*

(84) *Faster, Higher, Stronger.*

(85) *Michael Jordan. In nine seasons with the Chicago Bulls, Jordan averaged 32.3 points per game, 2.2 more than runner-up Wilt Chamberlain.*

(86) *The Pittsburgh Steelers' Franco Harris.*

(87) *Dwight Clark. In the final minute of play, Clark's leaping catch in the end zone gave the San Francisco 49ers the victory over the Dallas Cowboys.*

(88) *Honus Wagner. In a 1990 auction, Los Angeles Kings owner Bruce McNall and star player Wayne Gretzky bid a record $450,000 for the early-twentieth-century card, which was pulled from production after Wagner opposed the use of his likeness to advertise tobacco products.*

**89.** *Romania's Nadia Comaneci.*

**90.** *Although the number is still issued today, Ernie Davis, Jim Brown, and Floyd Little are the most famous players to don number 44 for the Orangemen.*

**91.** *Jackie Robinson. After starring in baseball, football, and track at UCLA, Robinson debuted with the Brooklyn Dodgers at the age of 28 in 1947, and in 10 major league seasons he posted a career batting average of .311. He was inducted into the Hall of Fame in 1962.*

**92.** *Pitcher. Ruth broke in with the Boston Red Sox as a pitcher in 1914 and actually led the American League in ERA two years later before being converted to an outfielder in order to take advantage of his booming bat.*

**93.** *Sonja Henie. She took home the gold medal in 1928, 1932, and 1936.*

**94.** *Three consecutive strikes.*

**95.** *Indiana University. Led by Kent Benson and Quinn Buckner, the Hoosiers posted a perfect 32–0 record during the 1975–76 season.*

**96.** *Cassius Clay. Clay later changed his name to Muhammad Ali.*

**97.** *Bob Hayes. After winning the gold medal in the 100-meter dash at the 1964 Summer Olympics, Hayes starred for the Cowboys from 1965 to 1974.*

**98.** *He is the only pitcher in major league history to throw two consecutive no-hitters. In 1938, while pitching for the Cincinnati Reds, Vander Meer no-hit the Boston Braves, 3–0, on June 11 and duplicated the feat with a 6–0 no-hitter against the Brooklyn Dodgers four days later. Interestingly, the second no-hitter was also the first night game ever played at Brooklyn's legendary Ebbets Field.*

**99.** *None. Only three-year-old horses are allowed to race in the Derby.*

(100) *Named after its inventor, it is the machine used to resurface the ice at skating rinks.*

So how'd you do? If you didn't get them all, don't worry. While we think that every true sports fan *should* be able to answer all these questions, we didn't think many of you actually would. If you got 90 out of the 100, congratulations! You obviously know your stuff. And if you did get all 100 right (without looking anything up), give us a call. We may need somebody like you to help edit our next book. On the other hand, if you struggled to score a 65 on this test, you're obviously in need of some remedial reading. And the best way to brush up on the basics is to start by going back to school with Challenge 1.

## CHALLENGE 1. BACK TO SCHOOL

(1) *The Division III finalists. The Amos Alonzo Stagg Bowl is the Division III national championship game.*

(2) *The New Orleans Superdome. In 1982, North Carolina defeated Georgetown, 63–62, for the national championship, and in 1993, the Tar Heels topped Michigan, 77–71.*

(3) *Billy Sims. In 1979, Sims lost the Heisman race to USC's Charles White, but he was still elected by the Detroit Lions with the first pick overall in the 1980 NFL draft.*

(4) *Virginia and Louisiana State. After losing their semifinal game to North Carolina, Virginia salvaged third place by topping LSU, 78–74.*

(5) *Tennessee. Under head coach Pat Summitt, the Volunteers won the national championship in 1987, 1989, and 1991.*

(6) *Arkansas.*

(7) *North Carolina.*

(8) *Iowa. The Hawkeyes are coached by the legendary Dan Gable, who posted a 118–1 record during his college career at rival Iowa State.*

(9) *New Jersey. Seton Hall is located in South Orange, New Jersey, about 12 miles from New York City.*

(10) *Alabama. Green Bay's Bart Starr won the award in Super Bowls I and II, while fellow Crimson Tide alumnus Joe Namath was MVP of Super Bowl III.*

(11) *Villanova. In 1985, Villanova was seeded 8th in the Southeast region after posting a 19–10 regular-season record, but the Wildcats walked away with the national championship by upsetting Big East rival Georgetown, 63–63, in the final game.*

(12) *The University of Kansas. In the 1988 national championship game, the Danny Manning–led Jayhawks defeated Big Eight rival Oklahoma, 83–79.*

(13) *Indiana State. In 1979, the Larry Bird–led Sycamores compiled a perfect 33–0 record before finally losing, 63–50, to Magic Johnson's Michigan State squad in the national championship game.*

(14) *Northwestern Louisiana. After Joe Delaney won the award with the Kansas City Chiefs in 1981, John Stephens followed suit with the New England Patriots in 1988.*

(15) *Frank McGuire. McGuire won 550 games overall in his 30-year career.*

(16) *They are the only six Division I players to average at least 20 points and 20 rebounds per game during their collegiate careers.*

(17) *They all jumped directly from high school to the pros, bypassing college completely.*

(18) *Roger Staubach. He won the Heisman as Navy's quarterback in 1963.*

(19) *Michigan. In 1903, led by head coach Fielding Yost and his "Point a Minute" offense, the Wolverines trounced Stanford, 49–0.*

(20) *USC. Since 1923, the Trojans have won the Rose Bowl 19 times, more than twice as many as runner-up Michigan, which has won seven.*

☞ *Stanford. The men's team won the tournament in 1942, while the women prevailed in 1990 and again in 1992.*

☞ *Bill Walton. In the 1973 final, Walton connected on 21 of 22 field-goal attempts as the Bruins beat Memphis State, 87–66.*

☞ *Lew Alcindor. He led the Bruins to three straight titles from 1967 to 1969 before changing his name to Kareem Abdul-Jabbar.*

☞ *Oklahoma. Under Wilkinson, the Sooners finished atop the final Associated Press poll in 1951, 1955, and 1956.*

☞ *Marcus Allen, Mike Rozier, and Barry Sanders. Allen rushed for 2,342 yards at USC in 1981, Rozier piled up 2,148 yards for Nebraska in 1983, and Sanders amassed 2,628 yards for Oklahoma State in 1988.*

☞ *Omaha, Nebraska.*

☞ *Oregon. In the championship game, the Ducks beat Ohio State, 46–33.*

☞ *Elvin Hayes. Hayes averaged 36.8 points per game for Houston during the 1967–68 season.*

☞ *Oscar Robertson.*

☞ *Marcus Allen. Allen won the award in 1981 as a running back for the USC Trojans.*

☞ *USC's O. J. Simpson. Beban won the award for UCLA in 1967.*

☞ *Fordham University. The Seven Blocks of Granite were the Rams' imposing offensive line, and included future coaching legend Vince Lombardi.*

☞ *Ohio State. They were Buckeyes together from 1960 to 1962.*

☞ *USC. The Trojans have won the College World Series a record 11 times, including 5 straight from 1970 to 1974.*

35. *LaSalle University. In 1954, Tom Gola led the Explorers to a 92–76 victory over Bradley in the NCAA championship game.*

36. *The Dukes. Located in Pittsburgh, Duquesne is a member of the Atlantic-10 Conference and the alma mater of former NBA star Norm Nixon.*

37. *Austin Carr. Carr broke Bill Bradley's record of 58 points set against Wichita State in the 1965 consolation game.*

38. *The University of Minnesota. Brooks led the Golden Gophers to national titles in 1974, 1976, and 1979.*

39. *Jim McMahon. McMahon was the starting quarterback for the Chicago Bears in Super Bowl XX.*

40. *Otis Sistrunk. Famed for his shaved head, he was one of only a handful of NFL players who never attended college.*

41. *The Mid-American Conference.*

42. *Notre Dame.*

43. *Loyola Marymount. After losing Hank Gathers to a heart attack during the Big West Conference tournament, the high-scoring Lions went on an improbable run during the NCAA Tournament before finally losing to eventual champion UNLV.*

44. *In order, Notre Dame's seven Heisman winners are Angelo Bertelli (1943), Johnny Lujack (1947), Leon Hart (1949), Johnny Lattner (1953), Paul Hornung (1956), John Huarte (1964), and Tim Brown (1987).*

45. *Auburn. Despite being on NCAA probation, Terry Bowden led the Tigers to a perfect 11–0 record in his first season as head coach.*

46. *Frank Leahy. In 13 seasons with the Fighting Irish, Leahy posted a record of 107–13–9.*

47. *The University of Georgia.*

48. *Cheryl Miller. Miller led USC to the national championship in 1983 and 1984.*

(49) *Minnesota State.*

(50) *Columbia University. On January 1, 1934, Columbia defeated Stanford, 7–0, in the Rose Bowl.*

## CHALLENGE 2. IN THE BEGINNING

(1) *Seattle. The Pilots joined the American League in 1969, but after just one season in Seattle they moved to Milwaukee and became the Brewers.*

(2) *Don Shula. Shula led the Colts to the NFL championship in 1968, but they were upset by the AFL's New York Jets in Super Bowl III, 16–7.*

(3) *The Winnipeg Jets.*

(4) *The Edmonton Oilers, the Quebec Nordiques, and the Hartford Whalers. Along with the Jets, they were absorbed by the NHL when the WHA folded after the 1978–79 season.*

(5) *The Minnesota Twins and the Texas Rangers. The original Senators moved to Minnesota in 1961, but were replaced by an expansion team with the same name. The expansion Senators then moved to Texas in 1972.*

(6) *The Baltimore Bullets. Monroe averaged 24.3 points per game that year on his way to the NBA Rookie of the Year Award. He was eventually traded to the New York Knicks in November of 1971 and was a member of the Knicks' 1973 NBA championship team.*

(7) *First base. Eddie Stanky was the Dodgers' regular second baseman in 1947, but when he was traded to the Boston Braves the following spring, second base became Robinson's position for the next five years.*

(8) *Nadia Comaneci. The first gymnast to record a perfect score of 10 in Olympic competition, she won three individual gold medals in 1976.*

9  *The PGA Golf Championship.*

10  *The Tampa Bay Buccaneers. Despite having won the Heisman Trophy the year before, Jackson shocked the Bucs by deciding to pursue a professional baseball career instead, and by the end of the 1986 season was playing for the Kansas City Royals. He eventually made his NFL debut with the Los Angeles Raiders in 1987, but his football career was cut short by a severe hip injury in 1991.*

11  *The Polo Grounds. The Mets played at the legendary home of the New York Giants during their first two seasons (1962 and 1963) before moving to Shea Stadium in 1964.*

12  *The Indianapolis Racers. Gretzky played eight games for the World Hockey Association's Racers in 1978 before being sold to the Edmonton Oilers.*

13  *Boston University. Pitino coached the Terriers for two seasons before moving on to Providence College, the New York Knicks, and, eventually, the University of Kentucky.*

14  *Indiana State. Wooden coached the Sycamores in 1947 and 1948.*

15  *Purdue. A three-time All-American, Wooden was named national player of the year in 1932, and is the only person to be inducted into the college basketball Hall of Fame as both a player and a coach.*

16  *Walter Alston. Alston managed the Dodgers from 1954 to 1976, leading the team to seven pennants and four world championships. He was succeeded in 1977 by the Dodgers' current manager, Tommy Lasorda.*

17  *Cleveland. The Rams spent ten seasons in Ohio overall, and won the NFL championship there in 1945.*

18  *The San Francisco 49ers and the Los Angeles Raiders. Located in San Francisco, Kezar Stadium was the home of the Raiders in their inaugural season, 1960.*

19  *The Washington Redskins. Before moving to Washington in 1937, the Redskins were known as the Boston Braves.*

☛ *Power Memorial. Alcindor played basketball there from 1963 to 1965.*

☛ *Wilt Chamberlain. Chamberlain played two seasons for the University of Kansas and one with the Harlem Globetrotters before joining his hometown Philadelphia Warriors in 1959.*

☛ *The United States Military Academy. After being named head coach at the tender age of 24, Knight compiled a 102–50 record in six seasons at Army, where one of his players was current Duke head coach Mike Krzyzewski.*

☛ *Tom Landry. After posting an 0–11–1 record in his 1960 debut, Landry went on to win two Super Bowls with the Cowboys before being fired by new owner Jerry Jones in 1989. At the time of his dismissal, he was the only head coach the team had ever known.*

☛ *Jim Mora. Currently the coach of the New Orleans Saints, Mora led the Philadelphia Stars to the USFL championship in 1984 and the Baltimore Stars to the title in 1985.*

☛ *Philadelphia and Kansas City. The Philadelphia Athletics were one of the American League's original eight franchises in 1901, but after 54 seasons there they moved to Kansas City, from 1955 to 1967.*

☛ *The Los Angeles Kings, Minnesota North Stars, Pittsburgh Penguins, Philadelphia Flyers, St. Louis Blues, and California Seals. Of those six teams, the Penguins and the Flyers are the only clubs that have won the Stanley Cup.*

☛ *The St. Louis Blues. In fact, thanks to a divisional structure that guaranteed that an expansion team would play for the Stanley Cup, the Blues reached the finals in each of their first seasons, but were swept each time by one of the league's "Original Six."*

☛ *New Orleans. The Jazz joined the NBA as an expansion team in 1974, but never posted a winning record while playing in New Orleans.*

**29.** The Arizona Cardinals. After four decades as the Chicago Cardinals, the team moved to St. Louis in 1960 and then to Phoenix in 1988.

**30.** Kentucky. Playing for legendary head coach Adolph Rupp, Riley was a starter on the Kentucky squad that lost to Texas Western in the 1966 NCAA championship game.

**31.** Georgia Tech. Heisman began coaching in 1893, when he led Oberlin College in its first year of varsity football to a perfect 7-0-0 record. The next year, Heisman coached Akron. He returned to Oberlin before going to Auburn University and, later, Clemson.

Georgia Tech was the next stop; at Tech, Heisman was 101-28-6 over a span of sixteen seasons, from 1904 to 1919, including a streak of three years, 1915 to 1917, in which the team was unbeaten—23-0-2. And in the middle of that streak, Tech beat Cumberland 222-0, college football's highest recorded score. Heisman also coached baseball and basketball at Tech, but it was football where he made his mark. He was considered an innovator, creating the center snap to replace rolling the ball, and he was considered the "father of the forward pass," a champion of that concept until the rules committee accepted it in 1906.

From Tech, Heisman went to his alma mater, the University of Pennsylvania, then to Washington and Jefferson College for a season, and finally to Rice University.

Heisman finished coaching with a career record of 184-68-16, spanning thirty-six years. After coaching, he accepted a position as director of athletics with the New York Downtown Athletic Club.

**32.** Rochester, New York. Originally known as the Rochester Royals, the team also made stops in Cincinnati, Kansas City, and Omaha, before finally settling in Sacramento.

**33.** The Denver Nuggets, Indiana Pacers, New Jersey Nets, and San Antonio Spurs all joined the NBA when the ABA folded in 1976.

**34.** The Toronto Blue Jays. Ainge batted .220 in three seasons with Toronto (1979-81) before deciding to concentrate on a professional basketball career instead.

☞ *The New York Yankees. In 1989, Sanders batted .234 with two home runs in 14 games for the Yankees.*

☞ *The Kansas City Athletics. Jackson played 35 games for the Athletics in 1967, the year before they moved to Oakland.*

☞ *The Boston Red Sox. Ruth played in Boston from 1914 to 1919, where he helped the Red Sox win their last three world championships. After leading the American League with 29 home runs in 1919, however, he was sold to the New York Yankees for a then-record $100,000.*

☞ *John McKay. McKay's Bucs finished their inaugural season with an 0–14 record.*

☞ *George Seifert. After taking over for the retired Bill Walsh in 1989, Seifert led the San Francisco 49ers to a 14–2 regular-season record and a 55–10 victory over the Denver Broncos in Super Bowl XXIV.*

☞ *The Quebec Nordiques. Quebec selected Lindros with the first pick overall in the 1991 NHL draft, but after failing to sign him, traded him to Philadelphia for Ron Hextall, Mike Ricci, Peter Forsberg, Steve Duchesne, Kerry Huffman, a first-round draft pick, cash, and future considerations.*

☞ *The Los Angeles Clippers. Originally known as the Buffalo Braves, the team moved to San Diego in 1978 and then to Los Angeles in 1984.*

☞ *Bob McAdoo (1973), Ernie DiGregorio (1974), and Adrian Dantley (1977).*

☞ *The Brooklyn Dodgers. Durocher managed Brooklyn for nine seasons (1939–46, 1948), and led them to the National League pennant in 1941.*

☞ *Northwestern. Parseghian posted a 36–35–1 record as coach of the Wildcats, but was 95–17–4 at Notre Dame.*

☞ *The New York Jets. Holtz led New York to a 3–11 record in 1976, his only season as an NFL head coach.*

☞ *Purple and gold. The Kings changed uniforms prior to the 1988–89 season, and now resemble the NFL's Los Angeles Raiders instead of the NBA's Los Angeles Lakers.*

**47** Oklahoma. Aikman broke his leg in his second game as a Sooner in 1986, then transferred to UCLA after the season.

**48** The New York Mets. Ryan posted a 6–3 record for the Mets in 1969, then added a save in his only World Series appearance as New York beat the Baltimore Orioles, four games to one.

**49** The Miami Dolphins. Miami went 3–11 in its inaugural year, but seven seasons later the Dolphins were Super Bowl champs.

**50** Wimbledon. It was first contested in 1877, four years before the inaugural U.S. Open.

## CHALLENGE 3. FAMOUS FIRSTS

**1** The Boston Red Sox. In 1903, the Red Sox upset the Pittsburgh Pirates, five games to three, and scored a huge victory for the upstart American League (which was founded in 1901) in their battle for equality with the more-established National League.

**2** Max McGee. Playing for the injured Boyd Dowler, McGee caught a 37-yard touchdown pass from Bart Starr midway through the first quarter to give the Green Bay Packers a 7–0 lead over the Kansas City Chiefs. McGee also caught another touchdown pass later in the game and finished with seven receptions overall as the Packers romped, 35–10.

**3** Cincinnati. Nicknamed the Red Stockings, the team barnstormed as professionals until the founding of the National League in 1876.

**4** The Winter Olympics. Prior to 1924, some events now in the Winter Games were held at the Summer Games instead.

**5** The Kentucky Derby.

**6** A goaltender's mask. Plante led the Montreal Canadiens to six Stanley Cup titles during the 1950s.

☞ Jay Berwanger. The University of Chicago star was selected by the Philadelphia Eagles just months after becoming the first Heisman Trophy winner as well.

☞ Curtis Strange. In 1988, Strange won a total of $1,147,644 and was named PGA Player of the Year.

☞ Jackie Robinson. Robinson won the inaugural award for the Brooklyn Dodgers in 1947, when only one player from both leagues was selected. Since 1949, a winner has been selected from each league.

☞ Larry Doby. Doby hit just .156 in 29 games for the Indians in 1947, but in 1948 he batted .301 as Cleveland captured baseball's World Series.

☞ St. Louis. In 1904, St. Louis was the site of both the Summer Olympics and the World's Fair.

☞ Ty Cobb. Cobb was named on 95 percent of the initial ballots, while runner-up Babe Ruth appeared on "only" 90 percent.

☞ Floyd Patterson. Patterson regained the title by defeating Ingemar Johansson in 1960, one year after losing it. He then surrendered the belt for good when he was knocked out in the first round by Sonny Liston in 1962.

☞ Ron Blomberg. On April 6, 1973, New York Yankee Blomberg drew a bases-loaded walk off of Boston's Luis Tiant in the first-ever plate appearance by a major league designated hitter.

☞ John Daly. Using a driver and a one-iron, Daly reached the green on his second shot, then two-putted for a birdie on the 630-yard hole. Unfortunately, he still finished the tournament in 33rd place with a total score of 284.

☞ Mike Garrett. Garrett won the award in 1965, three seasons before fellow Trojan O. J. Simpson.

☞ Marcus Allen. Allen rushed for 2,342 yards in 1981 while leading the Trojans to a 9–3 record.

**18** Carlos Baerga. In the seventh inning of a game against the New York Yankees, Baerga homered left-handed against Steve Farr and right-handed against Steve Howe, leading the Cleveland Indians to a 15–5 victory.

**19** Shaquille O'Neal (1992) and Chris Webber (1993). Orlando signed O'Neal, but they promptly traded Webber to the Golden State Warriors for the rights to Memphis State star Anfernee Hardaway.

**20** The Indianapolis 500. Ribbs qualified for the field of 33 in 1991, but failed to finish the race.

**21** Althea Gibson. Gibson defeated Darlene Hard in straight sets to win her first Wimbledon title in 1957, then defended her crown by defeating Angela Mortimer in straight sets in 1958.

**22** Jack Johnson. Johnson took the title by knocking out Australian Tommy Burns in Sydney on December 26, 1908.

**23** Connie Hawkins. Hawkins failed to report a bribe while at Iowa in 1962, but as the war between the rival leagues intensified, the NBA ban was lifted and Hawkins signed with the Phoenix Suns.

**24** Babe Ruth. In the inaugural game in 1933, Ruth christened the competition with a two-run home run in the third inning, leading the American League to a 4–2 victory at Chicago's Comiskey Park.

**25** Fred Lynn. In the 1983 All-Star Game, Lynn connected during a seven-run third inning against San Francisco's Atlee Hammaker as the American League cruised to a 13–3 victory. It was Lynn's fourth career, All-Star homer, tying him for second all-time behind Hall of Famer Stan Musial.

**26** Mike Ditka. Ditka played 12 seasons with the Chicago Bears and Dallas Cowboys before coaching the Bears to an NFL championship in Super Bowl XX.

**27** Jan Stenerud. Stenerud scored 1,699 points during his 19-year career, second on the all-time list behind kicker/quarterback George Blanda.

28. Hollywood Park. Wild Again, an 80–1 long shot, was the winner of the Breeder's Cup Classic in that inaugural year.

29. Akeem Olajuwon. Olajuwon was drafted by the Houston Rockets and the University of Kentucky's Sam Bowie was chosen by the Portland Trail Blazers before the Bulls plucked Jordan with the third pick overall in the first round.

30. The Philadelphia Flyers. In 1974, the Flyers defeated the Boston Bruins four games to two to win the Stanley Cup in only their eighth NHL season. Philadelphia also won the Cup again the following season by defeating the Buffalo Sabres, four games to two.

31. Figure skating. Salchow was the inventor of the backward, one-revolution jump that now bears his name.

32. The Phoenix Suns' Larry Nance.

33. Maureen Connolly. In 1953, Connolly won Wimbledon, the French Open, the U.S. Open, and the Australian Open, at the tender age of 19, but her career ended the following year when she was nearly killed in a riding accident.

34. George Mikan. Mikan led the Minneapolis Lakers to three straight NBA titles during the 1950s before taking over the fledgling ABA in 1967.

35. Tonya Harding. Harding landed the difficult jump during the 1991 U.S. Figure Skating Championships, where she upset Kristi Yamaguchi for the gold medal.

36. Penn State. The Nittany Lions upset defending champion UCLA in the finals, three games to two.

37. Julie Krone. Krone rode Colonial Affair to a two-length victory over Kissin' Kris in the 1993 Belmont Stakes.

38. He became the first NHL goaltender to score a goal.

39. Billy Kidd. Also the first American to be crowned world champion, Kidd won a silver medal in the slalom.

40. Phil Esposito. Esposito first cracked the 100-point barrier during the 1968–69 season, when he recorded 49 goals and 77 assists for 126 total points.

41 *Uruguay. The championship game was played in Montevideo, Uruguay's capital city.*

42 *Rex Chapman. The Hornets selected Chapman with the eighth pick overall in the 1988 NBA draft.*

43 *Garry Templeton. In 1979, Templeton led the National League with 211 hits overall while batting .314 for the St. Louis Cardinals.*

44 *The Houston Oilers. Blanda threw for 301 yards in the title game as Houston defeated the Los Angeles Chargers, 24–16.*

45 *The Los Angeles Rams.*

46 *ESPN. In the league's cable debut, the New York Giants defeated the New England Patriots, 17–10.*

47 *The New Orleans Superdome. In Super Bowl XIII, the Dallas Cowboys defeated the Denver Broncos, 27–10.*

48 *Joey Jay. Jay debuted as a pitcher for the Milwaukee Braves in 1953 and would go on to win 99 games during his major league career.*

49 *William Howard Taft. After christening the season for the Washington Senators, Taft watched Walter Johnson pitch a 1–0 one-hitter against the Philadelphia Athletics.*

50 *They were the first-ever winners in thoroughbred racing's three Triple Crown races. Aristides won the Kentucky Derby in 1875, Survivor took the Preakness in 1873, and Ruthless won the Belmont in 1867.*

## CHALLENGE 4. WE HARDLY KNEW YE

1 *Wally Pipp. Pipp actually led the American League in home runs in 1916 and 1917, but when he was sidelined by a headache one day in 1925, Gehrig took his place and didn't miss another game until 1939.*

☞ *Lorenzo Charles. After teammate Derek Whittenberg shot a desperation air-ball in the closing seconds, Charles caught the ball and dunked it at the buzzer to give the Wolfpack a 54–52 victory over the heavily favored Cougars.*

☞ *Gerard Phelan. With no time remaining, Phelan caught a 49-yard "Hail Mary" touchdown pass from eventual Heisman Trophy winner Doug Flutie to give BC a miraculous victory.*

☞ *Darryl Lamonica. Lamonica started for the Oakland Raiders in Super Bowl II, a 33–14 loss to the Green Bay Packers.*

☞ *Phil Bengston. Under Bengston, the two-time defending Super Bowl champions posted a 6–7–1 record.*

☞ *Timmie Smith. After rushing for just 126 yards during the regular season, Smith rumbled for 204 during Washington's 42–10 rout of the Denver Broncos in Super Bowl XXII. He played just two more seasons in the NFL, however, and gained only 612 yards in his entire career.*

☞ *Playing for the Chicago Cubs from 1906 to 1910, Steinfeldt was the overlooked third baseman in the infield that featured the legendary double-play combination of shortstop Joe Tinker, second baseman Johnny Evers, and first baseman Frank Chance.*

☞ *The tie-break system. Van Allen was a three-time U.S. singles champion, but his greatest legacy is his scoring system, which was first used in 1965 and was formally adopted by the United States Tennis Association in 1970.*

☞ *Ezzard Charles. On June 22, 1949, Charles defeated Jersey Joe Walcott to win the title that had been unclaimed since Louis's retirement.*

☞ *Elmore Smith. On October 28, 1973, Smith blocked 17 shots in a game against the Portland Trail Blazers. He went on to lead the league that year with an average of 4.85 blocks per game.*

☞ *Rick Wise. While playing for the Philadelphia Phillies on June 23, 1971, Wise pitched a no-hitter and slugged two* home runs to single-handedly beat the Cincinnati Reds, 4–0.

12. He became the first man ever to clear seven feet in the high jump.

13. He posed for the Heisman Trophy. Unfortunately, Smith did not know what he was posing for, and he did not realize that the trophy was his likeness until 1982, 47 years after the fact.

14. Bob Bender. After playing just one minute (and scoring no points) during the final game of Indiana's 1976 national championship season, Bender transferred to Duke and scored seven points in the Blue Devils' championship-game loss to Kentucky in 1978. He never played in the NBA.

15. Ken Hubbs. As a rookie in 1962, Hubbs batted just .260 with five home runs, but he did win a Gold Glove for his outstanding defensive play at second base.

16. Phoebe Mills. By capturing the bronze medal in the balance beam, Mills became the first U.S. gymnast to win a medal of any type at an "unboycotted" Olympics.

17. Willie Mays Aikens. In 1980 while playing for the Royals, Aikens homered twice in Game One and again in Game Four, but Kansas City still lost to Philadelphia, four games to two.

18. They all caught one of Nolan Ryan's seven no-hitters. Torborg, Kusnyer, Egan, and Rodriguez caught Ryan's four no-hitters with the California Angels, Ashby caught one with the Houston Astros, and Russell and Stanley caught Ryan's final two gems with the Texas Rangers.

19. Jack Twyman. Twyman averaged 31.2 points per game for the Cincinnati Royals, but finished second in the scoring race to Philadelphia Warriors rookie Wilt Chamberlain, who averaged 37.4.

20. Jim Taylor. Taylor rushed for 1,474 yards in 1962, while Brown managed only 996.

**21** *Francisco Cabrera. After collecting just three hits all season, Cabrera stroked a two-run single with two out in the bottom of the ninth to give the Braves a 3–2 come-from-behind victory over the Pittsburgh Pirates.*

**22** *Shawn Abner. Considered a "can't miss" prospect when he was drafted out of his Mechanicsburg, Pennsylvania, high school. Abner batted just .227 in five major league seasons.*

**23** *Roger Connor. A nineteenth-century star, Connor hit 138 home runs from 1880 to 1897.*

**24** *Bert Bell. Bell served from 1946 to 1959.*

**25** *England. In 1936, Perry defeated Baron Gottfried von Cramm, 6–3, 6–4, and 6–2.*

**26** *Harold Reynolds. With Henderson limited to only 95 games because of injuries, Reynolds led the league with 60 stolen bases for the Seattle Mariners in 1987.*

**27** *Mark Davis. Davis saved 44 games that year, then saved a total of 11 in the next four seasons.*

**28** *Randy Moffitt. Moffitt posted a 43–52 career record with the Giants, Astros, and Blue Jays.*

**29** *Scarpati was the holder when Tom Dempsey kicked his NFL-record 63-yard field goal that year.*

**30** *In Super Bowl I, Mercer kicked the game's first field goal when he connected from 31 yards out in the second quarter of Kansas City's 35–10 loss to the Green Bay Packers.*

**31** *Return a kickoff for a touchdown. Walker turned the trick for the Miami Dolphins in Super Bowl XVII while Jennings did it for the Cincinnati Bengals in Super Bowl XIII. Both, however, were in a losing cause.*

**32** *Dan Ross. In Super Bowl XVI, Ross, a tight end, caught 11 passes for the Cincinnati Bengals in a 26–21 loss to the 49ers.*

**33** *J. R. Richard. Richard was coming off of back-to-back 300-strikeout seasons and had led the National League in ERA* *the year before, but was felled by a stroke on July 30 and never pitched in the major leagues again.*

34 *Twelve years earlier, he won a gold medal in boxing at the Summer Olympics, making him the only Olympic athlete ever to win gold in both the Summer and Winter games.*

35 *Bill Fitch. Fitch coached Cleveland, Boston, Houston, and New Jersey for a total of 1,722 regular-season games from 1970 to 1992.*

36 *James "Buster" Douglas. On February 10, 1990, Douglas shocked the world by knocking Tyson out in the 10th round, but he lost the title to Evander Holyfield in his first defense eight months later.*

37 *The Boston Braves. Ruth played just 28 games for the Braves in 1935, but in his final week with the team, he did belt three home runs in one game against the Pittsburgh Pirates.*

38 *The Chicago Blackhawks. After 10 seasons with the Boston Bruins, Orr played two more years with Chicago before chronic knee problems forced him to retire.*

39 *The Washington Redskins. During their 1969 season, Lombardi led Washington to a 7–5–2 record, with his final game being a 20–10 loss to the Dallas Cowboys.*

40 *Tennis. Captained by Billie Jean King, The Freedom competed in World Team Tennis from 1971 to 1973.*

41 *Basketball. As members of the American Basketball Association, the Squires held the distinction of being Julius Erving's first professional team.*

42 *Soccer. The Tea Men competed in the North American Soccer League from 1977 to 1980.*

43 *George Foster. Foster slugged 52 homers for the Cincinnati Reds in 1977, then led the league again with 40 in 1978. He finished his career with 348 homers in 18 seasons.*

44 *Bob Lemon. Lemon began the 1978 season managing the Chicago White Sox, but after being fired midseason he was*

hired by the Yankees to replace Billy Martin and led New York back from a 14-game deficit to win both the pennant and the World Series.

☞ *The pole vault. Representing the United States, Richards won gold in 1952 with a vault of 14 feet, 11 inches, then defended his Olympic title with a vault of 14 feet, 11½ inches in 1956.*

☞ *Jimmy Qualls. Qualls batted .250 in 43 games for the Chicago Cubs in 1969, the season in which he collected 30 of his 31 career hits.*

☞ *George Plimpton. Renowned for his first-person looks at the world of professional sports, Plimpton's misadventures in the Detroit backfield were chronicled in the 1966 book* Paper Lion.

☞ *Eddie Edwards. Nicknamed "The Eagle," he finished the competition with less than half the points of his competitors.*

☞ *While pitching for the St. Louis Browns on May 6, 1953, Holloman tossed a no-hitter in his first major league start, blanking the Athletics, 6–0. Unfortunately for Holloman, the no-hitter was also his last career complete game, and by 1954 he was out of the major leagues for good.*

☞ *In the opening sequence of ABC's "Wide World of Sports," Bogataj was the ski jumper whose terrifying crash was used to illustrate "the agony of defeat."*

## CHALLENGE 5. BROKEN RECORDS

☞ *Walter Payton. Payton rushed for 110 touchdowns in 13 seasons with the Chicago Bears.*

☞ *Wayne Gretzky. Gretzky set the mark during the 1981–82 season as a member of the Edmonton Oilers.*

☞ *Bob Beamon. Beamon set the mark with a leap of 29 feet, 2½ inches at the 1968 Summer Olympics in Mexico City.*

4. His own. Ruth hit 59 home runs for the New York Yankees in 1921, giving him two of the top three home-run seasons in major league history.

5. Ty Cobb. Cobb collected 4,191 hits during his 24-year career, and was baseball's all-time hit king until switch-hitting Pete Rose overtook him during the 1985 season.

6. Tony Dorsett. With Dallas pinned on its own one-yard line, Dorsett sprinted 99 yards for a touchdown against the Minnesota Vikings.

7. Norm Van Brocklin. He set the mark on September 28 in a game against the New York Yanks.

8. Mickey Mantle. Mantle slugged 18 career World Series home runs, three more than runner-up Ruth. Jackson is tied for fifth place with 10.

9. Yogi Berra. Berra collected 71 hits in a record 75 World Series games. DiMaggio and Gehrig are in fourth and ninth places, respectively, with 54 and 43.

10. Whitey Ford. Ford posted a 10–8 record in 22 World Series appearances, making him the World Series record-holder in losses as well as wins.

11. Paul Hornung. In addition to scoring 15 touchdowns, Hornung kicked 41 extra points and 15 field goals for the Green Bay Packers.

12. Elgin Baylor. Baylor averaged 40.6 points per game in the 1962 finals, but the Lakers still lost to the Boston Celtics, four games to three.

13. The Cleveland Indians. In 1954, the Tribe won an amazing 111 games, but were swept in the World Series by the New York Giants.

14. Most career interceptions. Krause picked off 81 passes during his 16-year career.

15. Fran Tarkenton. Tarkenton threw for 47,003 yards in 18 seasons with the Minnesota Vikings and New York Giants, a distance of 26.7 miles.

☞ *Dan O'Brien. Despite failing to qualify for the U.S. Olympic team, O'Brien set the record with 8,891 total points during a meet at Talence, France. Dave Johnson did make the Olympic team and won the bronze medal with 8,309 points at Barcelona.*

☞ *Penalty minutes. Williams was banished to the box for 3,966 minutes during his 13-year career, giving him more than 16 times as many penalty minutes as goals (241).*

☞ *Most hits in one season. Sisler rapped 257 hits that year on his way to a .407 batting average.*

☞ *Hack Wilson. Wilson also set a National League record with 56 home runs that season, but the Cubs still finished second, two games behind the St. Louis Cardinals.*

☞ *Bobby Orr. The Norris Trophy is awarded to the league's top defenseman.*

☞ *Paul Coffey. Coffey tallied 48 times for the Edmonton Oilers during the 1985–86 season, breaking Bobby Orr's single-season record.*

☞ *Bobby Thigpen and Randy Myers. Thigpen set the major league record with 57 saves for the White Sox in 1990, while Myers set the National League mark with 53 for the Cubs in 1993.*

☞ *Wilt Chamberlain. During the 1959–60 season, Chamberlain averaged 37.6 points per game for the Philadelphia Warriors, the highest average in the league that season and, at the time, the highest average in NBA history.*

☞ *Ken Griffey, Jr. Griffey homered in eight straight games from July 22 to July 29, tying the record first set by Pittsburgh's Dale Long in 1956 and later equaled by the Yankees' Don Mattingly in 1987.*

☞ *Mark Whiten. Playing for the St. Louis Cardinals, Whiten also tied a record with four home runs that day as the Cards routed the Cincinnati Reds, 15–2.*

☞ *Don Hutson. Playing for the Green Bay Packers, Hutson led the league in scoring every season from 1940 to 1944.*

During that time, he also handled the Packers' kicking chores.

27 Lou Gehrig. *Before being felled by the disease that now bears his name, Gehrig belted 23 grand slams in his 17 major league seasons.*

28 Mike Marshall. *Marshall posted a 15–12 record with 21 saves for the Los Angeles Dodgers that season on his way to becoming the first reliever ever to win a Cy Young Award.*

29 The Philadelphia 76ers. *Their leading scorer that year was their current coach—Fred Carter.*

30 Dave Schultz. *Nicknamed "The Hammer," Schultz was one of the leaders of Philadelphia's "Broad Street Bullies," who won back-to-back Stanley Cup titles in 1974 and 1975.*

31 Babe Ruth. *Ruth actually accomplished the feat twice, in Game Four in 1926 and again in Game Four in 1928.*

32 John Riggins. *Riggins rumbled for 1,347 yards for the Washington Redskins that season, but the NFC champions were still overwhelmed by the Raiders in the Super Bowl, 38–9.*

33 Hank Aaron. *Aaron drove in 2,297 runs during his illustrious career, surpassing Babe Ruth's mark of 2,213.*

34 Eddie Mathews. *Mathews hit 452 of his 512 career home runs during his 13 seasons with Milwaukee. He also hit 25 in one season with the Boston Braves and 16 in one season with Atlanta.*

35 Ricky Watters. *He set the mark during San Francisco's 44–3 rout of the New York Giants.*

36 Rod Martin. *Martin intercepted Philadelphia's Ron Jaworski three times during the Raiders' 27–10 victory, giving him more successful catches than any of the Eagles' receivers!*

37 Darryl Sittler. *Sittler scored six goals and added four assists as Toronto routed Boston, 11–4. That game represented 10 percent of Sittler's scoring output for the entire season, as*

*he finished the year with 41 goals and 59 assists for exactly 100 points.*

☞ *The javelin. England's Steve Backley holds the record with a toss of 300 feet, 1 inch, 15½ feet farther than the world record in the hammer throw.*

☞ *The Milwaukee Bucks. On January 9, the Bucks beat the Lakers, 120–104, but Los Angeles still went on to win the NBA championship in five games over the New York Knicks.*

☞ *Franco Harris. Harris scored four Super Bowl touchdowns for the Pittsburgh Steelers during the 1970s, a feat later matched by San Francisco 49er teammates Jerry Rice and Roger Craig.*

☞ *Orel Hershiser. The consecutive-scoreless-inning streak started against Montreal in the sixth inning on August 30, 1988, and lasted through the tenth inning against San Diego on September 28.*

☞ *Terry Sawchuk. In 21 seasons with the Detroit Red Wings and the Toronto Maple Leafs, Sawchuk posted a record 103 shutouts.*

☞ *Dan Marino. In 1984, Marino led the Miami Dolphins to the AFC championship with 48 touchdown passes, 18 of them to Mark Clayton.*

☞ *Phil and Joe Niekro. The Niekros won 539 games during their major league careers (318 by Phil, 221 by Joe), 10 more than Gaylord (314) and Jim (215) Perry.*

☞ *Don Baylor. Before taking the reins of the expansion Colorado Rockies, Baylor was plunked 242 times during his 19-year career.*

☞ *Ron Hunt. A two-time All-Star, Hunt was hit by 243 pitches during his 12-year career, and led the National League a record 7 consecutive times.*

☞ *Phil Simms. In a 39–20 victory over the Denver Broncos, Simms completed 22 of 25 passes for 268 yards to lead the*

New York Giants to their first-ever Super Bowl championship.

(48) Don Sutton. Don Drysdale is in second place with 209.

(49) Mickey Mantle. Mantle played in 2,401 games during his
18-year career, all as a member of the Yankees.

(50) Willie Mays and Stan Musial. Both players were helped by
the fact that two All-Star Games were played each year from
1959 to 1962.

## CHALLENGE 6. NUMBERS UP

(1) Fifteen. Gehrig did not miss a single game between June 1,
1925, and May 1, 1939, but a mere two years after his
streak ended, he died of amyotrophic lateral sclerosis, which
is now more commonly called Lou Gehrig's disease.

(2) Seven. Ohio State is in second place with five, including two
by Archie Griffin.

(3) Eleven. Despite the addition of Penn State as a member in
1993, the conference decided to retain its original name.

(4) 126.

(5) Sixteen. The four division winners, plus the six teams with
the next-best records in each conference.

(6) Seven. Stengel led the Yankees to five straight titles from
1949 to 1953, plus 1956 and 1958. McCarthy's Yankees
won four in a row from 1936 to 1939, and also won in
1932, 1941, and 1943.

(7) None. Cobb retired after the 1928 season, five years before
the inaugural All-Star Game.

(8) Eight. It is one of 13 numbers the Yankees have retired,
more than any other team in the major leagues.

(9) 511. It is the number of home runs Ott hit during his career,
as well as the number of games won by baseball's winning-
est pitcher.

Fifty-four. Each team must make 27 outs, three per inning for nine innings.

Five. The plate is 17 inches wide and 17 inches deep.

9–0. One run for each inning.

2–0. It is the lowest possible score by which a team can win.

Five. In 22 All-Star Games, Rose played left field, right field, second base, third base, and first base.

Three. Montana led the Fighting Irish to college football's national championship in 1977.

Twelve. Every two years, the Ryder Cup pits the best golfers from the United States against their European counterparts in a three-day match-play competition.

Nineteen.

Twelve. The six division winners, plus three additional "wild-card" teams from each conference.

Lee Roy Selmon. In 1976, Selmon became the first player ever drafted by Tampa Bay, and as a defensive end, he starred for the Bucs until 1984.

Eight feet. Sotomayor broke the eight-foot barrier in San Juan, Puerto Rico, on July 29, 1989, and at the 1992 Summer Olympics he walked away with the gold medal despite jumping "only" 7 feet, 8 inches.

Five. Heiden swept the men's speed-skating events, winning gold at 500 meters, 1,000 meters, 1,500 meters, 5,000 meters, and 10,000 meters. The only other gold medal won by the United States in 1980 was by the hockey team.

One. Balls number one through eight are all solid colors. The nine ball is white with a yellow stripe.

Seven. Heptathletes compete in the 800-meter run, the 100-meter hurdles, the high jump, the shot put, the 200-meter run, the javelin, and the long jump.

**24** Five thousand. According to the poem:

> Then from 5,000 throats and more there rose a lusty yell;
> It rumbled through the valley, it rattled in the dell;
> It knocked upon the mountain and recoiled up the flat,
> For Casey, mighty Casey, was advancing to the bat.

**25** Ninety minutes. Each game consists of two 45-minute halves.

**26** One. Madden coached the Oakland Raiders to a 32–14 victory over the Minnesota Vikings in Super Bowl XI.

**27** Sixteen pounds, exactly the same weight as the men's shot put.

**28** Two hundred. Each lap is two and a half miles long.

**29** Five. Borg won Wimbledon each year from 1976 to 1980.

**30** Forty-seven. Three minutes per round, with a one-minute rest between each round.

**31** One. On their way to their 16th NBA championship, the Celtics were 40–1 at home and 27–14 on the road, with their only home loss coming December 6 against Portland.

**32** Fifty feet.

**33** Nolan Ryan and Steve Carlton. Carlton retired in 1988 with 4,136 career strikeouts, while Ryan retired in 1993 as baseball's all-time strikeout king with 5,714.

**34** Five. After being hired to manage the Yankees for the first time during the 1975 season, Martin was fired in 1978, re-hired in 1979, fired after the 1979 season, and rehired again for single seasons in 1983, 1985, and 1988. His only World Series championship as a manager came in 1977, when New York beat Los Angeles, four games to two.

**35** Gary McDermott wore number 32 in 1968, O. J. Simpson's rookie season with the Buffalo Bills.

**36** Lefty Grove. Grove posted a career record of 300–141 in 17 seasons with the Philadelphia Athletics and Boston Red Sox.

37 *Eric Dickerson. Dickerson rushed for 2,105 yards with the Los Angeles Rams in 1984, breaking Simpson's record of 2,003 for the Buffalo Bills in 1973.*

38 *Roberto Clemente. Clemente collected his 3,000th hit on the final day of the 1972 season, three months before dying in a plane crash while flying emergency relief supplies to earthquake victims in Nicaragua.*

39 *The Portland Memorial Coliseum, where the hometown Blazers have sold out every regular-season game since 1977.*

40 *None. The Jets defeated the Baltimore Colts 16–7 on the strength of three Jim Turner field goals and a four-yard touchdown run by Matt Snell. Namath, however, did complete 17 of 28 passes for 206 yards.*

41 *The Pebble Beach Golf Links is a par 72 course.*

42 *Three. The last All-Star to pitch more than three innings was the Kansas City A's Catfish Hunter, who pitched the final five innings of the American League's 15-inning loss in 1967.*

43 *The NHL. Hockey teams play a total of 84 games in the regular season, two more than their counterparts in the NBA.*

44 *Steve Garvey. After 14 seasons with the Los Angeles Dodgers, Garvey spent the final five years of his career in San Diego, and in 1984 led the Padres to their only World Series appearance.*

45 *Three feet.*

46 *Seventy-five percent. In 1992, Tom Seaver received the highest percentage of votes ever when he was named on more than 96 percent of the ballots.*

47 *Fifteen feet.*

48 *Twelve.*

49 *One-eighth of a mile. The term derives from the distance that a horse could plow a furrow in a field.*

(50) *Twenty feet. In 1991, Bubka became the first man ever to clear 20 feet both indoors and outdoors, but at the 1992 Summer Olympics he didn't even win a medal when he failed to clear his opening height.*

## CHALLENGE 7. THE NAME GAME

(1) *The California Angels, Minnesota Twins, and Texas Rangers. The Angels were originally known as the Los Angeles Angels, but they changed their name when they moved to Anaheim in 1966.*

(2) *The Baltimore Orioles, Toronto Blue Jays, and St. Louis Cardinals.*

(3) *Murderer's Row. With a lineup that featured Babe Ruth (.356, 60 home runs, 164 runs batted in), Lou Gehrig (.373, 47 home runs, 175 runs batted in), Earle Combs (.356), Bob Meusel (.337), and Tony Lazzeri (.309), the Yankees posted a record of 110–44 before sweeping the Pittsburgh Pirates in the World Series.*

(4) *Mark Fidrych. As a rookie in 1976, Fidrych was the American League's starting pitcher in the All-Star Game, but he was better known for his on-field antics, which included talking to the baseball and manicuring the mound with his bare hands. After winning 19 games as a rookie, however, he injured his arm and won only two more thereafter.*

(5) *Carl Hubbell. Hubbell won 253 games in 16 seasons with the Giants, but is best known for striking out five consecutive Hall of Famers in the 1934 All-Star Game.*

(6) *Tigers. In Division I basketball, there are 11 schools with that nickname, tying it for first place with "Eagles."*

(7) *Eric Dickerson and Craig James. Dickerson went on to set the NFL single-season rushing record with the Los Angeles Rams in 1984, while James reached the Super Bowl with the*

*New England Patriots before becoming a college football analyst for ESPN.*

(☞ 8) *Bruce Smith. The 1941 Heisman Trophy winner played at Minnesota, while the 1985 Bruce Smith starred at Virginia Tech.*

(☞ 9) *1969. The first two Super Bowls were actually called the AFL–NFL World Championship Game, but the name was changed for Super Bowl III, which saw the underdog New York Jets upset the heavily favored Baltimore Colts.*

(☞ 10) *John Riggins. Riggins began his career as a New York Jet, but he blossomed in Washington and finished his career with 11,352 yards rushing.*

(☞ 11) *Chuck Bednarik. A center and linebacker, Bednarik played for the Philadelphia Eagles from 1949 to 1962, but is best remembered for one vicious tackle that caused the New York Giants' Frank Gifford to miss the entire 1961 season.*

(☞ 12) *The Buffalo Bills. They earned their nickname by turning on "The Juice," opening holes for teammate O. J. Simpson.*

(☞ 13) *"The No-Name Defense." The Dolphins allowed just 171 points that season with a defense that featured linebacker Nick Buoniconti and safety Jake Scott.*

(☞ 14) *Walter Payton. Payton rushed for an NFL-record 16,726 yards in 13 seasons with the Chicago Bears.*

(☞ 15) *The Dallas Texans. The team was based in Dallas from 1960 to 1962.*

(☞ 16) *Red Grange. Grange was a three-time All-American at the University of Illinois before embarking on an NFL career with the Chicago Bears.*

(☞ 17) *"The Toe." In addition to his kicking duties, Groza also played tackle for the Browns.*

(☞ 18) *Jack "Hacksaw" Reynolds. Reynolds played 15 seasons in the NFL, earning a Super Bowl ring with the San Francisco 49ers in 1982.*

19 *Ken Stabler. "The Snake" led the Oakland Raiders to victory in Super Bowl XI.*

20 *Dick Lane. "Night Train" finished his career with 68 interceptions in 14 seasons.*

21 *The Arizona Cardinals, Atlanta Falcons, Philadelphia Eagles, and Seattle Seahawks.*

22 *"Crazy Legs." Hirsch played offensive end for the Los Angeles Rams from 1949 to 1957, catching 387 passes for 7,029 yards and 60 touchdowns.*

23 *Ron Jaworski. During the 1980 season, Jaworski led the Philadelphia Eagles to their only NFC championship, but in the Super Bowl he threw three interceptions (all by Rod Martin) as the Eagles lost to the Raiders, 27–10.*

24 *Patrick, Adams, Norris, and Smythe. Named for four of hockey's pioneers, the Lester Patrick and Charles Adams divisions were in the Prince of Wales Conference and the James Norris and Conn Smythe divisions were in the Clarence Campbell conference.*

25 *Bernie Geoffrion. As a player, Geoffrion won six Stanley Cups as a member of the Canadiens, and finished his career with 393 goals. He coached the Flames from 1972 to 1974.*

26 *Paavo Nurmi. As the world's dominant distance runner from 1920 to 1928, Nurmi won gold medals in the 1,500-, 5,000-, and 10,000-meter runs.*

27 *Minnesota Fats. He was the inspiration for Jackie Gleason's character in the Paul Newman classic,* The Hustler.

28 *Jets and Oilers. In the NFL, they play in New York and Houston, respectively, while the NHL versions hail from Winnipeg and Edmonton.*

29 *The Sacramento Kings and the Los Angeles Kings.*

30 *Leo Durocher. Durocher won 2,015 games in 24 seasons as a major league manager, and piloted the New York Giants to the world championship in 1954.*

31 The Utah Jazz, Orlando Magic, and Miami Heat.

32 The Tampa Bay Lightning.

33 Jackie Joyner-Kersee. Kersee's brother, Al Joyner, is Florence Griffith-Joyner's husband. All three are Olympic gold medal winners.

34 Bobby Hull. Known for the speed of both his skating and his slapshot, Hull scored 610 goals in 16 NHL seasons. His son Brett is currently a high-scoring star with the St. Louis Blues.

35 The St. Louis Cardinals. Led by player-manager Frankie Frisch, the rough-and-tumble Cardinals won the World Series in 1934.

36 Ahmad Rashad. A star receiver for the Minnesota Vikings from 1976 to 1982, Rashad changed his name after his rookie season with the St. Louis Cardinals in 1972.

37 The Crocodile. In addition to winning three French Open singles titles (in 1925, 1927, and 1929), Lacoste founded the clothing company that today bears both his name and the distinctive crocodile logo.

38 Wrestling. Better known as André the Giant, he died in 1993.

39 Cassius Clay (Muhammad Ali). Clay won the world heavyweight championship by knocking out Sonny Liston in 1964, but his cocky attitude and boastful, singsong rhymes irritated much of the boxing establishment.

40 Apollo Creed. Played by Carl Weathers, Creed retains his title with a 15-round decision in the original movie, then loses the crown in a rematch in Rocky II.

41 Indianapolis. Originally made of brick, the Indianapolis Motor Speedway is the site of the Indianapolis 500.

42 Arnie's Army.

43 Sumo wrestling. "Meat Bomb" is the nickname of the sumo wrestler Konishiki.

(44) *The Denver Broncos. Despite boasting an outstanding receiving corps in Ricky Nattiel, Mark Jackson, and Vance Johnson, the Broncos were routed by the Washington Redskins in Super Bowl XXII, 42–10.*

(45) *The Nasty Boys. In a four-game sweep of the Oakland A's that year, Reds relievers Norm Charlton, Randy Myers, and Rob Dibble had a contained ERA of 0.00.*

(46) *Pelé. Perhaps the world's most famous soccer player, he led Brazil to the World Cup title in 1958, 1962, and 1970.*

(47) *Leroy. Because of baseball's color barrier, Paige didn't reach the major leagues until age 42, but he was still inducted into the Hall of Fame on the basis of his outstanding career in the Negro Leagues.*

(48) Bull Durham. *Crash Davis was the perennial minor league catcher played by Kevin Costner.*

(49) *The U.S. Open tennis tournament.*

(50) *Chris Jackson. He changed his name prior to the 1993–94 season.*

## CHALLENGE 8. CHAMPS AND CHUMPS

(1) *Shoeless Joe Jackson. In 1911, Jackson's .408 batting average was second to Ty Cobb's .420, and his .356 career mark is third on baseball's all-time list behind Cobb and Rogers Hornsby.*

(2) *César Geronimo. Bob Gibson of the St. Louis Cardinals collected strikeout number 3000 on July 17, 1974, on a second-inning fanning of César Geronimo. Geronimo helped Nolan Ryan join the elite 3000 club when he fanned again six years later on July 4, 1980.*

(3) *Ernie Banks. Banks belted 512 home runs for the Chicago Cubs from 1953 to 1971, but the best finish his team could*

*muster was 92–70 in 1969, when they placed second behind the New York Mets.*

☞ *The Montreal Expos and the Houston Astros. Montreal lost the 1981 National League Championship Series to the Los Angeles Dodgers, three games to two, while the Astros lost the NLCS to the Philadelphia Phillies in 1980 and the New York Mets in 1986.*

☞ *The California Angels, Seattle Mariners, and Texas Rangers. Of the three teams, the Angels are the only one that has ever reached the playoffs, losing to the Baltimore Orioles in 1979, the Milwaukee Brewers in 1982, and the Boston Red Sox in 1986.*

☞ *Anthony Young. Luckless as both a starter and a reliever, Young's streak reached 27 before he finally beat the Marlins, 5–4, on July 28. The streak started on April 19, 1992.*

☞ *Sal Maglie. In his final World Series start, the former 20-game winner allowed just two runs on five hits, but wound up as a mere footnote to Larsen's historic performance.*

☞ *Roberto DeVicenzo. Runner-up Bob Goalby won the Green Jacket after DeVicenzo signed a scorecard that had been incorrectly filled out by his playing partner, an automatic disqualification.*

☞ *Greg Norman. In addition to losing in sudden death to Paul Azinger at the 1993 PGA Championship, Norman also lost playoffs to Fuzzy Zoeller at the 1984 U.S. Open, Larry Mize at the 1987 Masters, and Mark Calcavecchia at the 1989 British Open.*

☞ *The Cleveland Browns, Houston Oilers, Seattle Seahawks, and San Diego Chargers. Of those four teams, the Browns have come closest most often, losing three times in the AFC championship game.*

☞ *The Arizona Cardinals, Tampa Bay Buccaneers, Detroit Lions, New Orleans Saints, and Atlanta Falcons. Of those five teams, Tampa Bay is the only one ever to reach the NFL Championship Game.*

*Len Dawson. After losing to the Green Bay Packers in Super Bowl I, Dawson's Kansas City Chiefs beat the Minnesota Vikings, 23–7, in Super Bowl IV, with Dawson passing for 142 yards and one touchdown.*

*Dolphins kicker Garo Yepremian. With Miami leading 14–0 in the fourth quarter, Yepremian's foolish pass after a botched field goal attempt was intercepted by Mike Bass and returned 49 yards for a touchdown.*

*Jackie Smith. Dallas settled for a field goal on the drive and eventually lost the game, 35–31.*

*Dennis Conner. In 1983, Conner lost the Cup to the Australian entry skippered by John Bertrand, the first time a foreign boat had won since the competition began in 1851.*

*The U.S. Open and the Australian Open. Despite winning the French Open six times and Wimbledon five times, Borg lost all four of his trips to the U.S. Open finals and never even reached the finals in Australia.*

*Wimbledon. Lendl did reach the finals twice, but lost to Boris Becker in 1986 and Pat Cash in 1987.*

*The Washington Generals.*

*Sparky Anderson. After leading the Cincinnati Reds to back-to-back world championships in 1975 and 1976, Anderson led the Detroit Tigers to the title in 1984.*

*Ray Floyd. In 1992, Floyd won the Doral Ryder Open on the PGA Tour and also won three times on the Senior Tour.*

*The Dallas Cowboys. In nine Super Bowl appearances, the Cowboys have won four and lost five.*

*The Oakland Raiders. Oakland beat the Philadelphia Eagles in Super Bowl XV after finishing second behind the San Diego Chargers in the AFC West in 1980. Oakland and San Diego posted identical 11–5 records that season, but the Chargers were awarded the division title on a tiebreaker.*

*Joe Kapp. In addition to playing in the 1959 Rose Bowl with California and Super Bowl IV with the Minnesota Vik-*

*ings, Kapp also quarterbacked with Winnipeg Blue Bombers to two Grey Cups.*

☞ *Three. Walsh led the 49ers to victory in Super Bowls XVI, XIX, and XXIII before retiring. He then "unretired" to become head coach at Stanford University.*

☞ *Jimmy Johnson. After leading the Miami Hurricanes to the college football championship in 1987, Johnson led the Dallas Cowboys to back-to-back Super Bowl titles in the 1992 and 1993 seasons.*

☞ *Chuck Daly. Daly led the Detroit Pistons to back-to-back NBA championships in 1989 and 1990, and was also the coach of the U.S. Olympic "Dream Team" that captured the gold medal at Barcelona in 1992.*

☞ *John Taylor. Taylor caught a 10-yard pass from Joe Montana to cap a game-winning 92-yard drive late in the fourth quarter.*

☞ *Ron Turcotte. Turcotte also won two of the three Triple Crown races on Riva Ridge the year before.*

☞ *The Toronto Maple Leafs. Toronto has won 13 Stanley Cups, most recently in 1967.*

☞ *Finland. After upsetting the Soviet Union the game before, the U.S. beat Finland 4–2 in the final game to clinch the gold medal.*

☞ *Joe Frazier and George Foreman. Frazier captured the gold medal at Tokyo in 1964 while Foreman brought home the gold from Mexico City in 1968. Four other heavyweight champs also won Olympic gold medals, but in lower weight classes: Floyd Patterson and Michael Spinks were middleweights, while Cassius Clay and Leon Spinks were light heavyweights.*

☞ *England. England defeated West Germany, 4–2 in overtime, to win its only World Cup championship.*

☞ *Tracy Austin. Austin defeated Chris Evert Lloyd, 6–4, 6–3, to win the 1979 U.S. Open, then won the tournament again two years later by defeating Martina Navratilova.*

**34** *Leon Spinks. Spinks won the title with a 15-second split decision, but his reign was short-lived as Ali regained the belt by unanimous decision in a rematch seven months later.*

**35** *Rocky Marciano. After successfully defending his title six times, Marciano retired in 1955 with a career record of 49–0.*

**36** *The Lakers. Including their years in Minneapolis, the Lakers have reached the NBA finals a record 24 times, winning 10 and losing 14. The Boston Celtics have reached the finals 19 times, but once they get there they are an amazing 16–3.*

**37** *Ben Johnson. Johnson won the 100-meter dash in a sizzling 9.79 seconds, but when it was discovered that he had been taking performance-enhancing steroids, his name was expunged from the record book and his gold medal was given to runner-up Carl Lewis.*

**38** *Rosie Ruiz. Initially, Ruiz was crowned the winner, but when it was discovered that she did not run the entire race, first place was awarded to Canada's Jacqueline Garreau instead.*

**39** *Vic Wertz. Mays snatched a Wertz drive with two men on in a 2–2 tie in the first game of the World Series. There were no outs in the eighth inning when Wertz clocked it, and Mays's incredible throw—after the incredible catch— kept the runners to a one-base advance, preserving the tie so the Giants could win in extra innings!*

**40** *The Washington Redskins. After finishing with an 8–1 record in 1982, the Redskins went on to beat the Miami Dolphins in Super Bowl XVII, and after going 11–4 in 1987, they routed the Denver Broncos in Super Bowl XXII.*

**41** *The Dodgers. In 19 trips to the World Series, the Dodgers have won 6 and lost 13, 9 while in Brooklyn and 4 in Los Angeles.*

**42** *The New York Nets. Now based in New Jersey, the Nets defeated the Denver Nuggets four games to two for the final ABA title.*

☞ *Harvey Haddix. Pitching for the Pittsburgh Pirates, Haddix lost 1–0 to the Braves despite retiring Milwaukee's first 36 batters in order.*

☞ *The Baltimore Orioles. In 1980, the Orioles finished 100–62, three games behind the New York Yankees in the American League East.*

☞ *Bart Starr. Starr quarterbacked the Green Bay Packers to victory over the Kansas City Chiefs in Super Bowl I and the Oakland Raiders in Super Bowl II.*

☞ *Linford Christie. Christie covered the 100 meters in 9.96 seconds, supplanting Carl Lewis as "The World's Fastest Human."*

☞ *Kip Keino. Four years later, Keino struck gold again by winning the 3,000-meter steeplechase in 1972.*

☞ *Scott Hamilton. He was world champion from 1981 to 1984.*

☞ *John L. Sullivan. Renowned for the boast, "I can lick any man in the house!", Sullivan reigned as world heavyweight champ from 1882 to 1892, before finally losing to "Gentleman" Jim Corbett on a 21st-round knockout.*

☞ *Boris Becker. Becker was just 17 years old when he defeated Kevin Curren for the title, 6–3, 6–7, 7–6, and 6–4.*

**CHALLENGE 9. AND THE WINNER IS . . .**

☞ *Gaylord Perry. Perry won the American League award when he went 24–16 with a 1.92 ERA for the Cleveland Indians in 1972, then won the National League version with a 21–6, 2.72 mark for the San Diego Padres in 1978.*

☞ *Brooks Robinson. He won 16 straight for the Baltimore Orioles from 1960 to 1975.*

☞ *Fred McGriff. After leading the American League with 36 home runs for the Toronto Blue Jays in 1989, McGriff topped the National League with 35 for the San Diego Padres in 1992.*

☞ *Ozzie Smith. Entering the 1994 season, the "Wizard of Oz" had won 13 Gold Gloves for his outstanding defensive work. No other National League player has won more than 11.*

☞ *Bobby Richardson. Richardson batted .367 with 12 runs batted in, but New York still lost to the Pittsburgh Pirates on Bill Mazeroski's ninth-inning home run in Game Seven.*

☞ *Cal Ripken. Ripken won the award for the Baltimore Orioles in both 1983 and 1991.*

☞ *Keith Hernandez and Willie Stargell. Hernandez batted .344 with 105 runs batted in for the St. Louis Cardinals, while Stargell led the Pittsburgh Pirates to the World Series by slugging 32 home runs. Stargell was also named World Series MVP that year, as Pittsburgh beat the Baltimore Orioles, four games to three.*

☞ *Darrell Evans. The 38-year-old Evans slugged 40 home runs for the Detroit Tigers that year, three more than 36-year-old runner-up Carlton Fisk.*

☞ *The Baltimore Orioles. After being traded to Baltimore by the Cincinnati Reds during the off-season, Robinson hit .316 with 49 home runs and 122 runs batted in in 1966, leading the Orioles to their first-ever world championship.*

☞ *George Rogers. Rogers led the NFL with 1,674 yards rushing for the New Orleans Saints in 1981, just one season after leading the NCAA with 1,781 yards rushing at the University of South Carolina.*

☞ *Chuck Howley. With a pair of interceptions, Howley took home MVP honors in Super Bowl V, even though Dallas lost to the Baltimore Colts, 16–13.*

☞ *Ottis Anderson. Anderson rushed for 102 yards and one touchdown as New York defeated Buffalo, 20–19, the clos-*

*est the Bills have ever come to actually winning a Super Bowl.*

Bart Starr. *Starr won the first two Super Bowl MVP awards as the quarterback of the Green Bay Packers, and later coached the team for 10 seasons. Unfortunately, Starr never got near the Super Bowl as a coach, posting a career record of 52–76–3.*

Marcel Dionne. *Playing for the Los Angeles Kings, Dionne tied Gretzky for the scoring lead with 137 total points, but was awarded the scoring crown on the basis of more goals, 53–51.*

Bobby Clarke. *Clarke captured the Hart Trophy in 1973, 1975, and 1976, while the Flyers won the Stanley Cup in 1974 and 1975.*

Jerry West. *In the 1969 finals, West averaged 40 points per game for Los Angeles, but the Lakers still lost to their arch-rivals, the Boston Celtics, four games to three.*

Wes Unseld. *In 1969, Unseld averaged 13.8 points and 18.2 rebounds for the Baltimore Bullets, leading them to the Eastern Division championship with a 57–25 record. Without Unseld the year before, Baltimore had finished 36–46.*

Julius Erving. *After winning three straight ABA MVP Awards with the New York Nets from 1974 to 1976, Erving was traded to the Philadelphia 76ers and captured the NBA award in 1981.*

Larry Bird. *Bird owned the award from 1984 to 1986, during which time he led the Celtics to a pair of world championships.*

Kareem Abdul-Jabbar. *Winner of a record six MVP Awards overall, Jabbar won in 1971, 1972, and 1974 with the Milwaukee Bucks and in 1976, 1977, and 1980 with the Los Angeles Lakers.*

The Lady Byng Trophy. *Named after the wife of a former Canadian governor, the trophy was won a record seven times by New York Rangers center Frank Boucher.*

22. Rookies. Named after former NHL president Frank Calder, it is awarded to the league's Rookie of the Year.

23. Joe DiMaggio. DiMaggio set a major league record by hitting safely in 56 consecutive games that season, and his .357 batting average helped the New York Yankees win their ninth world championship. Williams, who was extremely unpopular with the writers who voted for the award, was also denied MVP honors in 1942 and 1947, despite winning the Triple Crown each year!

24. Florence Griffith-Joyner. "Flo-Jo" brought home the gold in the 100-meter dash, 200-meter dash, 4 × 100-meter relay, and the long jump.

25. Jennifer Capriati. Representing the United States, the 16-year-old Capriati came from behind to win the gold medal match, 3–6, 6–3, and 6–4.

26. Teofilo Stevenson. Unable to fight as a professional under Fidel Castro's strict regime, Stevenson dominated the amateur ranks by winning gold medals in 1972, 1976, and 1980.

27. Matt Biondi. Biondi captured 5 gold medals, 1 silver, and 1 bronze at Seoul, and has won a total of 11 medals overall in 3 trips to the Olympics.

28. Mario Andretti and A. J. Foyt. Andretti won at Daytona in 1967 and at Indianapolis in 1969, while Foyt won Daytona in 1972 to go along with his four Indy 500 championships in 1961, 1964, 1967, and 1977.

29. Grete Waitz. Despite Waitz's dominance, however, the race record-holder is Australia's Lisa Ondieki, with a time of 2:24:40.

30. Bill Rogers. Rogers also won the race in 1975, but the all-time leader is Clarence DeMar, who won his seventh Boston Marathon in 1930.

31. Bjorn Borg. Borg won each year from 1978 to 1981 and finished his career with six French Open championships overall.

☞ *Rod Laver. Laver captured all four major events in both 1962 and 1969.*

☞ *Chris Evert. Evert won six U.S. Open titles altogether.*

☞ *Sebastian Coe. Coe won gold at both Moscow (1980) and Los Angeles (1984), setting an Olympic record in 1984 with a time of 3:32.53.*

☞ *The Los Angeles Dodgers. The remarkable run of rookies included Rick Sutcliffe (1979), Steve Howe (1980), Fernando Valenzuela (1981), and Steve Sax (1982).*

☞ *Rick Sutcliffe. Sutcliffe was 4–5 with the Cleveland Indians when he was traded to the Chicago Cubs on June 13, 1980. He then went 16–1 the rest of the season to lead the Cubs to the Eastern Division championship and win the National League Cy Young Award.*

☞ *Hal Newhouser. Pitching for the Detroit Tigers, Newhouser was named AL MVP in 1944 and 1945 while most of the league's stars were off serving in World War II.*

☞ *Joe Montana. Montana captured the award in 1982, 1985, and 1990.*

☞ *Bobby Orr. After leading the NHL with 120 points in 1970, Orr duplicated his feat with 135 in 1975. As of 1994, he is still the only defenseman ever to win the NHL scoring title.*

☞ *The 100-meter dash, 200-meter dash, 4 × 100-meter relay, and the long jump.*

☞ *Seve Ballesteros. At age 23, Ballesteros was just two months younger than Jack Nicklaus was when Nicklaus won the Green Jacket in 1963.*

☞ *Al Kaline. Kaline was only 20 years old when he hit .340 for the Detroit Tigers that season.*

☞ *Mike Schmidt. Schmidt belted 548 home runs in 18 seasons with the Philadelphia Phillies, including a high of 48 in 1980.*

☞ *Alex Johnson. Johnson led the league with a .329 average in 1970, percentage points ahead of runner-up Carl Yastrzem-*

ski. Former Angel Rod Carew won eight batting titles during his career, but all eight came as a member of the Minnesota Twins.

(45) Sammy Baugh. "Slingin' Sammy" led the Redskins to the NFL championship in 1937 and 1942.

(46) Dominique Wilkins. During the 1985–86 season, Wilkins led the NBA with a 30.3 average for the Atlanta Hawks.

(47) Nate Archibald. Nicknamed "Tiny," the six-foot Archibald averaged 34.0 points and 11.4 assists for the Kansas City–Omaha Kings during the 1972–73 season.

(48) Swen Nater. Nater led the ABA with a 16.4 average for the San Antonio Spurs in 1975 and later topped the NBA with 15 rebounds per game for the San Diego Clippers in 1980.

(49) Rick Barry. After leading the NBA with 35.6 points per game for the San Francisco Warriors in 1967, Barry won the ABA scoring title with a 34.0 average for the Oakland Oaks in 1969.

(50) None. In fact, no Crimson Tide player has ever finished higher than fifth in the Heisman voting.

## CHALLENGE 10. GRAB BAG

(1) The Toledo Mud Hens.

(2) Red. Yellow cards are used to issue a warning, with two yellow cards equaling one red.

(3) Surfing. The movie by Bud Brown follows three surfers as they search for the perfect wave, which they eventually find at Cape St. Jefferies, South Africa.

(4) The mint julep. It consists of Kentucky bourbon over ice with sugar and a mint sprig.

☞ *The hand. One hand equals four inches.*

☞ *Cal Hubbard. After attending Centenary College in Louisiana, Hubbard became a four-time All-Pro in the NFL and eventually an American League umpire for 16 seasons.*

☞ *Madison Square Garden. First held in 1908, the meet moved to Madison Square Garden in 1914, and is one of the United States' premier indoor track events.*

☞ *Scotland. The course is St. Andrew's, where the rules of golf were first recorded in 1744.*

☞ *Tiger Stadium. Originally called Navin Field and later Briggs Stadium, it opened in 1912. Wrigley Field, which was originally called Weegham Park, opened in 1914.*

☞ *The Houston Astrodome. Remarkably, the stadium that was once dubbed "The Eighth Wonder of the World" seats only 50,496 fans for football.*

☞ *Flyweight. The maximum weight of a flyweight boxer is 112 pounds, compared to 118 for bantamweights, 126 for featherweights, and 135 for lightweights.*

☞ *Bill Buckner and Steve Sax. Buckner collected 201 hits for the Chicago Cubs in 1982 and again as a Boston Red Sox in 1985, while Sax collected 210 hits for the Los Angeles Dodgers in 1986 and 205 for the New York Yankees in 1989.*

☞ *Ten feet. It is exactly the same height as the rim in basketball.*

☞ *Fred Lynn and Lynn Swann. Swann caught four passes for 161 yards in the Pittsburgh Steelers' 21–17 victory over the Dallas Cowboys, while Lynn batted .331 with 21 home runs and 105 runs batted in for the American League champion Boston Red Sox.*

☞ *Pittsburgh and Philadelphia. Due to a player shortage, the Steelers and Eagles merged for the 1943 season.*

☞ *The Green Bay Packers. They play at both Lambeau Field in Green Bay and County Stadium in Milwaukee.*

**17** *The Buffalo Bills. The New York Jets and the New York Giants both play their home games at Giants Stadium in East Rutherford, New Jersey.*

**18** *Arizona. It is the name given to the group of major league teams that hold their spring training camps there instead of Florida. Florida teams make up the Grapefruit League.*

**19** *Hank and Tommie Aaron. Together, they belted 768 career home runs—755 by Hank and 13 by younger brother Tommie. Joe, Dominic, and Vince DiMaggio are in second place with a combined total of 574.*

**20** *George and Ken Brett. Third baseman George batted .390 with 24 home runs that season, while pitcher Ken recorded just one save in 13$\frac{1}{3}$ innings.*

**21** *Bud Greenspan.*

**22** *Rawlings.*

**23** *The Detroit Red Wings. When the NHL had only six teams, the eight legs of the octopus represented the eight playoff victories necessary to win the Stanley Cup.*

**24** *Dave McNally. In Game Three of the 1970 World Series, McNally belted a grand slam off of Wayne Granger in the sixth inning as Baltimore defeated the Cincinnati Reds, 9–3. Baltimore went on to win the series, four games to one.*

**25** *Table tennis. A sandwich bat is a paddle that has both sponge and rubber on its surface instead of just rubber.*

**26** *Eighteen.*

**27** *Lou Gehrig and Roberto Clemente. Both players had their careers cut short by tragedy, Gehrig by illness and Clemente by a fatal plane crash.*

**28** *Sandy Koufax. Five years after being forced to retire due to arthritis, Koufax was inducted in the Hall in 1972 at the tender age of 35.*

**29** *Babe Ruth. Gary Cooper played Lou Gehrig in the 1942 classic.*

☞ *Rice Stadium. Located in Houston, it was the site of Super Bowl VIII, in which the Miami Dolphins beat the Minnesota Vikings, 24–7, before 71,882 fans.*

☞ *The Metrodome. Located in Minnesota, it hosted the World Series in both 1987 and 1991, and Super Bowl XXVI in 1992. The only other stadiums to host events are the Los Angeles Coliseum (Super Bowls I and VII, plus the 1959 World Series) and San Diego's Jack Murphy Stadium (Super Bowl XXII and the 1984 Series).*

☞ *Sportsman's Park. In the only all–St. Louis World Series, the Cardinals defeated the Browns, four games to two.*

☞ *Melbourne, Australia. Melbourne hosted the 1956 Summer Games.*

☞ *Willie Mays. Mays was only 24 when he belted 51 home runs for the New York Giants in 1955, and he was 34 when he hit 52 for the San Francisco Giants in 1965.*

☞ *George Brett. Brett led the American League by batting .333 in 1976, .390 in 1980, and .329 in 1990, all with the Kansas City Royals.*

☞ *Gerald Ford. He was the star center that season for a team that posted a dismal 1–7–0 record.*

☞ *George Bush. He was the starting first baseman on a team that lost to USC in the finals of the College World Series.*

☞ *Dallas Green. In 1966, Green was pitching for the New York Mets when he surrendered Rose's only career grand slam. Fourteen years later, he managed Rose's Philadelphia Phillies to the 1980 world championship.*

☞ *Draw. For lefties, a draw (or hook) will move from left to right, the same as a fade (or slice) for right-handed golfers.*

☞ *Nancy Lopez. To be eligible for the LPGA Hall of Fame, a golfer must have played 10 years on the Tour and won either 30 tournaments with two majors, 35 tournaments with one major, or 40 tournaments with no majors.*

**127**

**41** Bob Watson. Watson hit for the cycle in both leagues. On June 24, 1977, as a Houston Astro, he pulled it off against San Francisco and was 4-for-4 in the 6–5 win. Two years later, as a Boston Red Sox, he did it again against the Orioles as he went 4-for-5 in a 10–2 victory.

**42** Bo Jackson. Before seeing his football career cut short by a hip injury, Jackson exploded for a 91-yard run against the Seattle Seahawks on November 30, 1987, and a 92-yard dash against the Cincinnati Bengals on November 5, 1989.

**43** Ken Stabler and Boomer Esiason. Stabler started Super Bowl XI for the Oakland Raiders, while Esiason started Super Bowl XXIII for the Cincinnati Bengals.

**44** The Preakness. The middle leg of the series is 1³/₁₆ miles, ¹/₁₆ of a mile shorter than the Kentucky Derby and ⁵/₁₆ shorter than the Belmont Stakes.

**45** Sapporo, Japan.

**46** Squaw Valley, California. At the 1960 Winter Olympics, the U.S. Olympic hockey team won the gold medal there, just as it did at Lake Placid twenty years later.

**47** The pentathlon. Patton finished fifth in the five-event pentathlon, which featured swimming, fencing, horseback riding, running, and shooting.

**48** Cricket. In baseball parlance, the bowler is the equivalent of the pitcher and the wicketkeeper is the equivalent of the catcher.

**49** Hershey, Pennsylvania. The Warriors occasionally played games outside Philadelphia to increase fan interest, and on that night, 4,124 fans watched Wilt make history in a 162–147 victory.

**50** Roller Derby.